Finding God in Each Moment

This marvelous book makes classic Ignatian discernment accessible in post-9/11 experience by providing a guide for finding God's will in the multi-layered network of relationships in which we live.

Janet M. O'Meara, Ph.D.
Professor of Religious Studies, Clarke College

This thorough and practical guide to the process of continuous spiritual discernment can transform relationships and turn intention into action on a daily basis.

Margaret Silf
Spiritual writer and retreat facilitator in the Ignatian tradition

In our overly busy world, making daily life a prayer has become ever more important. Drawing from Ignatian spirituality, this valuable volume provides clear and down-to-earth guidance for those seeking to live in the presence of God.

Bernard Cooke
Author of *Power and the Spirit of God*

This is a rare, careful, intelligent, systematic approach grounded in relationships and always conscious of the larger social context that is the true arena of God's formative work with each of us. It is a treasure trove of enlightening texts and wise, experienced guidance.

James E. Hug, S.J.
President of the Center of Concern

Finding God in Each Moment

The Practice of Discernment
in Everyday Life

Carol Ann Smith, SHCJ   Eugene F. Merz, SJ

Art by Joanne Emmer, C.S.J.

ave maria press  notre dame, indiana

© 2006 by Wisconsin Province of the Society of Jesus and Society of the Holy Child Jesus—American Province

All rights reserved. No part of this book may be used or reproduced in any manner whatsoever, except in the case of reprints in the context of reviews, without written permission from Ave Maria Press®, Inc., P.O. Box 428, Notre Dame, IN 46556.

Founded in 1865, Ave Maria Press is a ministry of the Indiana Province of Holy Cross.

www.avemariapress.com

ISBN-10 1-59471-100-3   ISBN-13 978-1-59471-100-8

Cover and text design by Katherine Robinson Coleman.

Cover photo © Laurie Rubin/Masterfile.

Printed and bound in the United States of America.

Library of Congress Cataloging-in-Publication Data

    Smith, Carol Ann S.H.C.J.

    Finding God in each moment: the practice of discernment in everyday life / Carol Ann Smith, Eugene F. Merz.

      p. cm.

    ISBN-13: 978-1-59471-100-8 (pbk.)

    ISBN-10: 1-59471-100-3 (pbk.)

    1. Discernment (Christian theology), 2. God—Omnipresence. 3. Spiritual life. 4. Spirituality. 5. Ignatius of Loyola, Saint, 1491-1556. I. Merz, Eugene. II. Title.

    BV4509.5.S623 2006

    218.4'82—dc22

                    2006007996

As we wrote Finding God in Each Moment, *tragedy after tragedy unfolded in the world around us. We were aware of both natural causes and human decisions which contributed to the suffering of so many people.*

We were inspired by the people whose decisions eased the suffering and often began the process of constructing a new world. The women, men, and children who lost their lives during this time were constantly in our prayer, and so we offer this book in their memory.

We invite others to prayerfully discern their decisions as responses to God's cry for justice so that life, not death, may result from our decisions.

Contents

Introduction

The generous and faithful God in our lives is One whose very lifeblood is relationship. When that vibrant trinitarian life of mutual self-gifting is shared with us in baptism, we too are caught up in the world of relationships. Relationships become our home away from Home, always revealing something of God's action and invitation to walk in God's light. Relationships are also the primary place within which discernment in our daily life takes place. This is true for all of our relationships—relationships with God's gifts in the created world, with friends, spouses, family members, colleagues, neighbors, committee members, cities, and nations. Above all, our relationship with God is itself a reality calling for discernment.

Our first book, *Moment by Moment: A Retreat in Everyday Life* set the stage in our hearts for this book. For many years we have heard women and men ask for help in living out the graces of *The Spiritual Exercises of St. Ignatius* after their retreat. In reality, they were asking for help with discernment, how to attend to the Spirit as she is poured out in their relationships and daily lives. We learned from the many people who used *Moment by Moment* that a simple structure to support one's prayer and to provide a process for discernment in one's daily life would be a helpful tool. Spiritual directors and retreat directors also told of their need for such a resource.

We recognize that a book of this type on discernment can serve as only one response among the many which are needed as we all move into a markedly new era characterized by globalization, cultural shifts, and very different groundings in the Christian faith tradition. Psychologists are also vital resources for the ongoing efforts to distinguish desolation from depression. Pastoral theologians, too, are critical to passing on an understanding of Christian faith without which our interpretation of our experience cannot rest on a solid foundation. Thus, responses that will enhance leadership, religious education, faith formation, and the psychological well-being of individuals and groups will come from other fields and surely will be important helps to our becoming discerning people. We hope that *Finding God in Each Moment* will bring new awareness of the Spirit's challenging life and consoling presence in the midst of our relationships at whatever age or place we find ourselves.

The primary structure of the book—the stages in relationships—is taken from what we have learned from listening to women and men speak of their struggle in relationships to be discerning, faithful, and just. At the heart of this book is our suggestion that our growth in justice will occur as we make our way with discerning hearts through the spiritual stages that constitute the growth in any relationship: Encounter,

Identity, Intimacy, Confrontation, Conversion, Reconciliation, Communion, Commitment, and Mission. The primary relationship within which this growth occurs is our personal relationship with God. To refuse the challenge contained in any successive stage in our relationship with God or with others is to risk superficiality rather than depth, stagnation rather than growth. Each stage holds the opportunity to discern God's presence and action there and to be "taught by God." The experiences within any relationship will always be the occasion of grace, even if they seem out of sync and catapult us to a different stage—whether with others or with God.

Our relationship with God, for all of its personal uniqueness and variety, seems to unfold in stages. This book calls those stages "Moments of Love." Each stage holds its own gift and challenge through which God is also teaching us how to be faithful to the responsibilities of the relationship. Fidelity to these responsibilities is an expression of justice. As the stages unfold in our relationships, a pattern emerges which gives evidence of the presence and action of God who is always calling us to grow and to become more loving and just. When patterned upon the identity of Jesus, relationships reveal the shared life of the Spirit active among us. Relationships become the place where believers make choices and decisions that help them grow in faith, in freedom, and in justice. Discernment helps us to navigate our way through those decisions and to bring them into harmony with God's loving action and hope for the world.

One's growth in discernment is always embodied in one's multiple relationships. Thus *Finding God in Each Moment* gives attention to the ways in which the needed dispositions for discernment are developed as we move through the stages in our relationships. Discernment can be a resource for us as we make the often hard choices required by the call to justice, that call to be faithful to the responsibilities of our many relationships. Contemporary Ignatian discernment requires that we be attuned to the needs and requirements of justice within our concrete situation when engaged in discerning a particular decision.

We have attempted to focus attention in simple ways upon the various dispositions which are the growth points within the dynamic movement in every healthy, mutual, growing relationship. While God is not limited to these ways in calling us to grow, these dispositions of heart and mind seem to be ones that are needed throughout the process of discernment. There does seem to be a usual sequence in which a person deepens in each of the qualities. Even though one may attend to the dispositions in a sequence, it is when they are taken together and lived as part of one's decisions and responses that the profile of the just and discerning person emerges.

Finding God in Each Moment invites you into an experience of ongoing reflection and prayer about the relationships in your life and the call to justice within them. It invites you to dip into your personal experience by means of questions that can both reveal and challenge your growth as a discerning and just person. While it is always helpful to reflect about one's faith journey with a spiritual director, we recognize that there are a limited number of qualified spiritual directors available in some places. That has been the case throughout history, and so people have turned to other wise women and men of faith who have listened, asked clarifying questions, and offered the encouragement and challenge found in scripture and in the "best practices" of many disciplines, professions, and walks of life. Such spiritual conversation is invaluable to one's growth in discernment.

St. Ignatius treasured spiritual conversation. He gave a significant place to such conversations as a form of ministry which he described as "any other ministration whatsoever of the word of God" (formula of the Institute of the Society of Jesus). In *The Autobiography*, Ignatius described the various ways in which he was taught by God through spiritual conversations and he envisioned spiritual conversation as part of the progression of the experience of *The Spiritual Exercises*. Throughout our lives, we have experienced the powerful action of God teaching and leading us through spiritual conversations. These conversations have revealed God's presence and action in the lives and hearts of the many women and men who have shared their faith experiences with us. "'And they shall all be taught by God.' Everyone who has heard and learned from the Father comes to me" (John 6:45). With them and though them, we have truly been "taught by God."

Our desire has been to present a clear, user-friendly and engaging text that will help people of faith and maturity become more discerning in their relationships. Such prayerful reflection is for the sake of making good choices in one's own sphere of influence, thus extending one's commitment to justice. All of us are challenged almost daily to ask where, in the face of so many needs and issues, we shall put our time, our talent, our wisdom, and our financial resources. We seek to know how we can stay attuned to the needs and changes in a global community without becoming overwhelmed and paralyzed into inaction. We can be caught in the apparent dichotomy between prayer and action and can fall prey as well to the temptation to separate the reality of our relationships from our efforts to become just persons and to do the just thing. *Finding God in Each Moment* invites us to consider that our relationships— with God, self, family, neighbor, community, nation, church, globe, creation—are the very places in which we daily discern the choices that will make us more just.

Finding God in Each Moment offers a practical structure for the prayer and reflection which must ground discernment. It offers suggestions for praying with the Word of God as well as some inspiration from two

Ignatian resources for practicing the art of discernment. *The Autobiography* of Ignatius shows a human being grappling with new awarenesses of the Spirit within his life and being. *The Spiritual Exercises* carry the supporting attitudes and values for a discerning life. They also contain Ignatius' two sets of "Rules for Discernment."

In addition to using material from scripture and the heritage of Ignatian spirituality, we have tried to incorporate some Vatican Council II statements which show elements of discernment at work as the Church expresses its concern for justice in the basic issues of mission, collaboration, work, cultural sensitivity, gender equity, and respect for the dignity, freedom, and gifts of all people. We hope that prayerful consideration of this "justice spin" on discernment may lead all of us to experience our choices and decisions as part of the global human response to God's cry for justice. The triune God continually invites us to become more aware of God's creation as a circle of life in which we all must share responsibly.

Faith leads us to trust that God, who is faithful and just, makes us faithful and just. Throughout any relationship and any process of discernment, we will be challenged to growth in faith. Christian faith is the foundation for all discernment; it is the air we must learn to breathe. Faith offers the final interpretation of the movement of God's Spirit within and among us. The life, death, and resurrection of Jesus Christ is the lens through which we must view the many patterns and dynamics which occur as we develop discerning lives.

May we pray often for the faith, hope, and love that ground wise discernment. May we grow in our trust that the source of our strength and hope is, simply and profoundly, in trusting and calling upon God, who is already present to us and constantly working in our midst. The justice of God shown in Jesus the Christ is and will remain the wellspring for our efforts and labors to be just women and men, "to act justly, love tenderly and walk humbly with our God" (Micah 6:4).

> The spirit of the Lord is upon [us], because he has anointed [us] to bring good news to the poor. He has sent [us] to proclaim release to the captives and recovery of sight to the blind, to let the oppressed go free, to proclaim the year of the Lord's favor (Luke 4:16–19).

May this text be fulfilled in our relationships today.

How to Use This Book

Finding God in Each Moment is designed to open you to a growing awareness of how God is actively forming you to be a more discerning person, of how you are being taught by God. It highlights the role of your human relationships as the experiential context within which to discern God's presence and activity. It suggests that within those same relationships you will experience opportunities to act justly, in the spirit of Vatican Council II, thus becoming a more discerning participant in our contemporary world. Becoming a more discerning person must also mean becoming a more just person. *Finding God in Each Moment* is a contribution to your lifelong journey of becoming more attentive to the faithful action of God in your life. While *Finding God in Each Moment* is neither a textbook nor a handy kit for a discernment process, it may be a resource for spiritual directors.

Moments of Love

The book is divided into nine "Moments of Love" which describe what we have discovered to be the spiritual stages through which any healthy, growing relationship will move: Encounter, Identity, Intimacy, Confrontation, Conversion, Reconciliation, Communion, Commitment, and Mission. The cumulative unfolding of these stages marks the faith-filled growth in all our relationships, whether they be with God, with another person, within a group, and even in our attitudes toward the world in which we live. A relationship may progress through these nine stages several times, but each time at a deeper level. Thus it is possible to find oneself at different stages in different relationships.

The Discernment Process

The important aspects in the process of discernment (Reflection on Experience, Prayer and Examen, Consolation and Desolation, Interior Freedom, Struggle and Choice) are described in separate features. We have placed them throughout the book in such a way as to break open their importance and significance to growth in discernment. Each description is followed by a few reflection questions to help one attend to that aspect of discernment. We would encourage you to spend some time in prayer and reflection with these questions as they appear before moving to the subsequent section. The "Profile of a Discerning Life" will help you to notice the discerning heart which is emerging within you as you grow.

Before beginning to pray with *Finding God in Each Moment*, it would be wise to consider how, in a significant relationship, especially in your relationship with God, you have already experienced moving through at least some of the stages and learning the ways of God. For example, you might consider your relationship with your spouse or a good friend and recall when you first met (Encounter), how you shared your self-understanding with each other (Identity), and how that sharing led you to an experience of trust, openness, honesty, and vulnerability (Intimacy). Your memories will also include times in which you were challenged to face some truth about yourself or the other (Confrontation) and how that led you to a change of attitude or behavior (Conversion) and a new place of forgiveness (Reconciliation) and mutual understanding (Communion). From that new place in the relationship, decisions about new ways of being or acting emerged (Commitment) and you gave yourself for others more generously (Mission).

The verification of the stages in your own personal experience will help you to understand how the book aims to be a support to you in any of the stages. It will also alert you to the fact that God is actively teaching you to be a more faithful and just disciple. One may begin *Finding God in Each Moment* with the first moment in any relationship—the Moment of Encounter—and gradually pray your way through to the Moment of Mission. Or, one may begin with the moment which seems to best describe where you are in a particular relationship and make your way from there. Praying with a particular Moment may also be of help at different significant moments in your life, for example, at a time when you are feeling confronted or when you are feeling called anew to conversion or when surprised by the gift of a new person in your life. Our hope is that you will be led to experience God drawing you through the convergence of all of those relationships. We hope that you, too, will experience yourself being "taught by God."

The Preludes

There is a prelude for each "Moment of Love", or stage in developing relationships. It offers a brief description of the experience of the stage and of the qualities which seem to be needed in that stage. The scripture quoted on each prelude page is always taken from two stories of profound personal religious experience: the Annunciation Mary's Story (Luke 1:26–41) and The Emmaus Story (Luke 24:13–35). Both stories capture God's mysterious presence and action as people move through a human conversation and event. The citation selected for each Moment shows the Moment's dynamic at work within those scriptural stories. Those scriptural narratives are intended to ground your prayer and reflection in the belief that God is acting at every stage of our human journey in relationships.

Qualities

Within each stage of one's relationship certain qualities are significant in the discernment process. To help you become more aware of God's action as you grow in each quality, we have offered a brief description of the quality, a grace to be prayed for, a quote from Ignatian material and some scripture passages for your prayer. A quotation from a document of Vatican Council II draws attention to the church's invitations to become more discerning and just. Appendix 2 lists the abbreviations and full titles of the documents of Vatican Council II.

Finally, for each quality there is a set of reflection questions that are meant to guide your reflection on how the quality is developing within all of your relationships. These questions could be used to bring all of your relationships to God in prayer.

A Specific Experience of Discernment

Finally, the book ends with a simple presentation of a way to move through a specific experience of discernment when making a particular, important decision. Hopefully, your experience of praying with the earlier parts of the book will have deepened in you the qualities of heart and mind that are necessary prerequisites for using discernment to make an important decision. In the Appendix, "Discernment as a Process for Personal Decision Making," you will find a brief presentation of a practical way of structuring your approach when discerning a significant matter in your life. This approach reflects the wisdom about decision making found in *The Spiritual Exercises*. The reflection questions may be helpful at each step in that process.

The reflection questions that accompany each quality not only provide a focus for prayer but also a focus for conversation with the other person or in a group as you try to be attentive to God's action and thus more discerning in the relationship. The questions also serve to help individuals and groups as they engage in reflection, prayer, and conversation about responding with a discerning heart to the critical needs of the world. Your own creativity and discernment may lead you to use *Finding God in Each Moment* in many other ways.

Our Experience of Being Taught by God

"Writing another book?" This question, often posed to us in jest, initially brought only a gasp of surprise from us. We thought our first book, *Moment by Moment*, was our last book! The prospect of writing another book took on a different significance when the editorial director at Ave Maria Press, Robert Hamma, suggested that we consider a book on the Examen prayer which has its origin in *The Spiritual Exercises of St. Ignatius*. Our response to that inquiry was that the Examen was really an aspect of discernment. Thus, God sows the seed!

As months passed, we became aware that much of what we had been hearing from women and men of faith was their need for some practical help with understanding and practicing discernment of spirits. So, with this need more clearly focused for us, we began some conversations about "a book on discernment" and a new phase of *our* journey of being "taught by God." A full narrative of that journey is beyond our gifts for comic relief, but it does seem that a presentation of the insights and convictions which grew in us and which form the background for *Finding God in Each Moment* may be of some value to those who pray with this book.

As spiritual directors, we are honored by those who share with us their experience of being in relationship—at home, at work, in school, in the community, in the church, in our nation, and in the world. Increasingly, women and men are pondering their relationship with all of creation. As we have listened, and as we have reflected upon the relationships within our own lives, we have noted that the journey is not totally idiosyncratic. There are stages through which relationships move and our relationship with God is often mirrored by our human relationships. Increasingly, God's cry for justice has found an echo in our human struggle to be just women and men.

Regardless of how large the justice issue may be, it will be addressed by people acting in relationship with each other—whether in world parliaments, in senate hearings, in city budget committees, in parish councils, at picnics, in university committees, in religious congregations' chapter meetings, or in the varied activities within personal households. In any of those settings, we are called by God to be faithful to the responsibilities of the relationships. Such human fidelity is a significant aspect of fidelity in our relationship with God who, in loving us first, has begun the relationship with us which is our very life.

Such human fidelity to the responsibilities of our multiple relationships is a significant arena for the practice of justice. Justice, flowing from the truth of our identity in relationship with and before God, extends beyond the basic requirements of contractual giving and taking. Justice is always fidelity in giving to another what is his or her due, but it is more than that. It is a way of being with others which calls forth openness, honesty, trust, integrity, fidelity, empathy, compassion, and understanding wherever people are brought together in relationship. We have noticed that not only do people grow in a consciousness regarding justice and injustice, but they also experience a gradual movement to a place of new understanding. The new understanding not only includes awareness of injustice within their own life, whether as actor or as recipient, but it also includes an awareness of their complicity in injustice and a fuller recognition of the opportunities for just action within their particular sphere of influence and action. Careful, sensitive discernment is important during that process of becoming a more just person.

Fidelity to the responsibilities of our relationships shapes our practice of justice, making it a consistent part of our lives. There is a history to this practice of justice. In the Hebrew scriptures, especially in the description of the covenant between Yahweh and Israel, we see justice as a style of being, of action, of life always in relationship to another. The justice of God is God's fidelity to the covenant promises shown in the deeds of salvation performed lovingly by Yahweh on behalf of Israel. Jesus' life, death, and resurrection are the revelations of God's justice shown now in human form. Jesus' proclamation of his mission makes clear his concern for justice:

When he came to Nazareth, where he had been brought up, he went to the synagogue on the Sabbath day, as was his custom. He stood up to read, and the scroll of the prophet Isaiah was given to him. He unrolled the scroll and found the place where it was written: "The Spirit of the Lord is upon me, because he has anointed me to bring good news to the poor. He has sent me to proclaim release to the captives and recovery of sight to the blind, to let the oppressed go free, to proclaim the year of the Lord's favor." And he rolled up the scroll, gave it back to the attendant, and sat down. The eyes of all in the synagogue were fixed on him. Then he began to say to them, "Today this scripture has been fulfilled in your hearing" (Luke 4:16–21).

These words capture the mission of Jesus in very simple words: to reveal the justice of God through relationships. Jesus also experienced the Spirit moving and leading him throughout his life. Sharing the mission of Jesus is also our call, our privilege, and our responsibility. Each one of us shares in this mission of Jesus: to reveal the justice of God through fidelity in our relationships. We must then, in the words of the poet e.e. cummings, "be of love (a little) More careful Than of everything" (*No Thanks,* 1935 manuscript).

Love alone is the energizing force capable of sustaining justice. The gift of God's Spirit is the source for that kind of love. To be a just person, respecting the rights and dignity of another, is to enter into loving solidarity with this person in all the moments of mutual relationship. The just person is one who, like Abraham, Job, Ruth, Amos, Mary, Joseph the carpenter, is recognized not simply by reason of what she/he did and said, but because of the fidelity of their total life in relationship to God and to other people. Our hope to be just people rests ultimately on God's steadfast fidelity toward a sometimes unfaithful Israel and toward us. In a word, God's justice is a gift, an activity manifesting God's faithfulness and love, thus restoring us, who are sinners yet loved, to goodness and life. This justice, this fidelity to the process and responsibilities of relationships, requires ongoing discernment of and response to the presence and action of God's Spirit in our multiple relationships. Faith leads us to trust that God who is faithful and just makes us faithful and just. Throughout any relationship and any process of discernment, we will be challenged to grow in faith.

We live in a relational world. The tragic events of September 11, the natural disasters that continue to occur around the world, as well as events unfolding in each of our own cities or towns, graphically reveal this truth. We are not self-sufficient individuals requiring nothing but God in order to exist. We are not individuals for whom community is optional. The reality is that we are social beings who live interdependently. Relationships constitute the very stuff of our natural and historical existence, both as individuals and as societies. We are nurtured and affected by relationships and derive energy and meaning from them. Relationships and the call of justice within them form the steady, ongoing context for our daily discernment.

Since the problematic character of our existence also flows, in large part, from relationships, they will always include struggle and suffering. Struggle often reveals deeper needs and questions. Discernment will not remove struggle or suffering from relationships, but our efforts to bring a discerning heart to them will minimize the conflictual aspects of the struggle. It will orient us so that the suffering is truly transformative. Our shared global experiences offer the potential and resources for dealing creatively with what could otherwise, in a moment, become a new manifestation of injustice.

Discernment can be a significant resource for us as we make our way through the daily complexities that confront us. We have the opportunity and responsibility to initiate and strengthen, to develop and support just relationships within the many contexts in which we live—families, colleagues, church communities, civic groups, classrooms, hospitals, boardrooms, and sports arenas. At its core, attending to such responsibility is a basic commitment to the solidarity of the human race. We are born into community. We depend upon relationships.

Relationships have a cost. The cross of Jesus reminds us of this. To "suffer" relationships is to bear, to endure, and to support them, trusting that God will redeem and re-create them. The call to justice and fidelity will include loss and letting go as part of bringing new life to the world of relationships. Sharing in the faith journey of other people has taught us that giving daily care to our relationships, and to the divine life and hope that they carry, is also an essential daily action for justice.

Drawing upon a Tradition

Among the amazing gifts God has given us is the capacity to recognize our experience of God. Throughout the tradition of Christian spirituality, women and men have offered the Christian community their insights about the experience of God which has guided and sustained them as they went about their lives and work in a relational world. They have spoken of images of God, of the word of God to them, of the struggle of being faithful to their experience of God, and of the joy in the practice of virtue that flowed from their experience of God.

The Autobiography of Ignatius offers his narrative of his experience in very human circumstances. It demonstrates his growing conviction that he was being taught, formed, and led by God within those very events. Within *The Spiritual Exercises*, Ignatius of Loyola offered his wisdom and insights for *interpreting* one's experience of God by means of the discernment of spirits. Like the saints before and after him, Ignatius had a passion for doing the will of God. This hunger to respond to the desires of God made him want to be able to recognize God's activity within him so he could unite his desires to God's desires. Ignatius wanted to notice the evidence that occurred in his own affectivity when he was moved by God. Then he could distinguish that evidence from the evidence of other spirits which could also be at work within him. Gradually, as he reflected upon his experience of God in prayer, in activity, and in relationships, Ignatius discovered some patterns within his interior experience. The guidelines, now known as "The Rules for Discernment of Spirits," are the articulation of those patterns.

A tradition only stays alive through many ages when it is re-expressed in the idiom of each particular age. The tradition of discernment as a guide for Christian living and decision making has deep relevance for people in our world today. However, this centuries-old practice needs to be re-appropriated in concrete and practical ways as we attend to our responsibilities as citizens of a global world and church. We are constantly faced with concrete and practical decisions about injustices. Without such a re-appropriation and re-expression, discernment will be found only in pious exercises or in volumes waiting passively on our bookshelves.

Ignatius' insights on discernment were not the first to be offered to the Christian community, but they are unique in the way in which they guide us in the *process* of discernment. In the "Rules for Discernment of Spirits," as throughout *The Spiritual Exercises*, Ignatius gives first place to God's action within the person.

Ignatius recognized that, while God's action is unique within each of us, the effects of that divine action follow some recognizable patterns. After five hundred years of experience with the "Rules for Discernment," many women and men see that those recognizable patterns have some universal applicability. Today, many are drawing upon the wisdom in the Rules not only within a retreat setting, but also within the context of daily life, moment by moment.

Observations from Our Experience

As we have watched people engage their own experience of God and relationships at times with fidelity and faith, at other times with struggle and doubt, we have noted that these two questions emerge over and over again: "How can I know what God is asking? How can I know God's will?" This pattern is the same for people who have prayed for many years and for people who have just begun to take seriously their personal relationship with God. Our awareness of the pattern has been heightened in recent years as we have listened to people who have been bombarded by a multiplicity of options in every dimension of their lives. Some have tried to have or do it all, only to discover a resulting inauthenticity in their lives. Others have turned to rules and laws in making choices only to discover that the vast majority of our daily choices fall not within the legal arena, but within the arena of the heart where the Spirit deftly guides us.

As members of a global family with developing international relationships, we are keenly aware that no one leader or group of leaders can take the place of God and give perfect answers to guide those who turn to them with questions. "Now concerning love of the brothers and sisters, you do not need to have anyone write to you, for you yourselves have been taught by God to love one another" (1 Thessalonians 4:9).

Indeed, like Ignatius, we are all being "taught by God." While God's ways may not always be our ways, God's ways are recognizable in their daily manifestations. They are God's way of forming us in the likeness of Christ. They are God's way of caring for the totality of creation that God loves so dearly.

Discerning God's Ways

Grounded in one's personal relationship with God, spiritual discernment is a gift, an art, and a skill. It is an experience of being formed and moved by God. It requires a disposition to receive, a sensitivity of mind, heart and body, and some clarity about its components. Solomon's prayer for a discerning heart in 1 Kings 3:9–12 reminds us to pray for the gift of discernment. The renewal of the practice of spiritual direction has focused attention on skills that empower us for discernment. However, skills also have their foundation in the good gifts that God has given us. Such gifts include education, mentoring, and practice. These gifts offer the "value-added" component that may lead, with God's further help, to wisdom. To each of these—art, skill, and gift—we must contribute open minds and hearts, and a humble hunger to discover God at work in us. Discovering God's work in each of us is the first step in discovering God's work in our world. With our minds and hearts formed to be increasingly discerning in our everyday lives and relationships, we will become more open and active in regard to local and world issues that cry out for the attention and care of just women and men.

Implementing a Vision of Justice

Vatican Council II (1962–1965) is a wonderful memory for some and a vague reference point for others. Vatican II repeatedly called women and men to become more aware and responsive to their share in the mission of Jesus, to live a life of faith that does justice. Reading the documents from the perspective of discernment has made us aware that the documents of Vatican II truly demonstrate the statements of a discerning body trying to be in relationship with God, with itself, and with others in the world. While not perfect in every aspect of discernment, the church speaks often in these documents as a body already moving to be discerning in its pursuit of justice. The church's overarching encouragement to one who is pursuing justice is to be discerning in one's approach.

As we revisit, practice, and live the wisdom in the council documents from the perspective of discernment, we may find ourselves having a new experience of a relational community. It is an experience of sharing life, reflecting upon it, and making a common judgment about it so that committed action may flow from the shared experience (cf. Bernard Lonergan, S.J., *Method in Theology*, p. 79). The themes of Vatican II provide an underlying disposition for thinking with, in, and for the church. Our hope is that the inclusion of some Vatican II statements in this book will encourage those who are trying to become more discerning to also become more attentive to Vatican II's cry for justice in all the relationships that make up life on our shared planet. In our time, attentiveness to the themes of the council is a critical disposition to develop in order to move with the Spirit in the world.

THE DISCERNMENT PROCESS: REFLECTION ON EXPERIENCE

Therefore I prayed and understanding was given me; I called on God, and the spirit of wisdom came to me (Wisdom 7:7).

The process of discerning God's gracious will in our lives begins with an attentive reflection upon our experience of prayer, relationships, and activity, especially decision making and actions for justice. In all of that experience, God is speaking to us and revealing to us who God is and how God is acting in our midst. Reflection upon experience is different from "thinking about it" or "processing it." The difference flows from the faith attention which guides the reflection. Faith leads us to look at our unfolding experience from the perspective of God's presence and action in all of creation and in all of us.

As we begin the process of discernment, we need to make a commitment to step back from the often intense pace of our lives in order to reflect. In reflection we recall the events of the recent past—a day, a week, a month—and ask the Spirit to guide us to an awareness of the presence and action of God within us and within those events. This search for the definite, and perhaps delicate, traces of God's action requires practice. Fidelity to this search deepens our desire to find God in all things and gradually leads to a recognition of the graced themes and patterns unfolding within one's relationship with God. Ignatius's words about the experience of consolation which occurs in us without apparent cause offers us wisdom:

> For often during this later period we ourselves act either through our own reasoning which springs from our own habits and the conclusions we draw from our own concepts and judgments, or through the influence of either a good or an evil spirit. In this way we form various projects and convictions which are not coming immediately from God our Lord. Hence, these need to be very carefully examined before they are fully accepted or carried into effect (*Spiritual Exercises*, Rules for Discernment, 336).

Reflection Questions

- How can I incorporate reflection on experience into my daily routine?
- Do I want to make that commitment even if it means that I will need to eliminate something else?
- What is the best time and place for me to reflect?
- What external factors help me to be faithful to a process of reflecting upon my experience?
- What doubts do I have about beginning my growth in discernment with daily reflection on God's presence and action in my life?

Select a favorite scripture passage that can call you to this daily reflection.

MOMENT *of* ENCOUNTER

Mary's Story

In the sixth month the angel Gabriel was sent by God to a town in Galilee called Nazareth. . . .

~LUKE 1:26

The Emmaus Story

Now on that same day two of them were going to a village called Emmaus, about seven miles from Jerusalem, and talking with each other about all these things that had happened. While they were talking and discussing, Jesus himself came near and went with them. . . .

~LUKE 24:13–15

God's ever-creative love continually moves among us, inviting us into deeper relationship with God through relationship with others. Mysteriously, one's relationship with God sheds light upon one's relationships with others. Perhaps surprisingly, our human relationships hold the potential for new understandings of being in relationship with God. As our relationships unfold, a process of personal transformation occurs. Honesty is essential in all relationships and all discernment.

Each encounter is a gift, like a seed yielding profoundly new possibilities in our lives. Discernment is one way of attending to God's call to us in an initial encounter. In this moment of Encounter, stillness, openness, awareness, and recognition of one's religious experience are qualities to develop as the gift unfolds.

Stillness

● ● ● ● ● ● ● ● ● ●

When freed from the pressures of noise and the demands on our time, stillness attunes our minds and hearts to notice within us the mysterious presence and action of God.

Ignatian Insights

"Part of the time he [Ignatius] spent in writing and part in prayer. The greatest consolation he experienced was gazing at the sky and the stars, which he often did and for long, because he thus felt within himself a very great impulse to serve our Lord. He often thought about his intention and wished he were now wholly well so he could get on his way [to Jerusalem]" (*Autobiography*, 11).

"By being secluded in this way [seeking moments of stillness] and not having our mind divided among many matters, but by concentrating instead all our attention on . . . the service of our Creator and our own spiritual progress, we enjoy a freer use of our natural faculties for seeking diligently what we so ardently desire . . . and the more we unite ourselves to him in this way, the more do we dispose ourselves to receive graces and gifts from his divine and supreme goodness" (*Spiritual Exercises*, 20).

"By a time of tranquility I mean one when the soul is not being moved one way and the other by various spirits and uses its natural faculties in freedom and peace" (*Spiritual Exercises*, 177).

Grace

To allow myself to be drawn into a quiet interior space and to bring that stillness to my relationships.

Scripture

"Be still, and know that I am God!" (Psalm 46:10).

"He said, 'Go out and stand on the mountain before the LORD, for the LORD is about to pass by.' Now there was a great wind, so strong that it was splitting mountains and breaking rocks in pieces before the LORD, but the LORD was not in the wind; and after the wind there was an earthquake, but the LORD was not in the earthquake; and after the earthquake a fire, but the LORD was not in the fire; and after the fire a sound of sheer silence" (1 Kings 19:11–12).

"But this I call to mind, and therefore I have hope: The steadfast love of the LORD never ceases, his mercies never come to an end; they are new every morning; great is your faithfulness. 'The LORD is my portion,' says my soul, 'therefore I will hope in him.' The LORD is good to those who wait for him, to the soul that seeks him. It is good that one should wait quietly for the salvation of the LORD. It is good . . . to sit alone in silence . . ." (Lamentations 3:21–28).

Reflection Questions

CONSIDERATIONS FOR PRAYER

- Am I comfortable in silence? What are the effects of solitude on me?

- If I am uncomfortable in silence, what can I do to address the cause of my discomfort?

- What are my memories of times of stillness in my life?

- What images of God have come to me at times when I have been still?

Further Resources

Psalm 46:10

Psalm 131

Ecclesiastes 3:1, 7

Exodus 14:14

Luke 10:38–42

DISCERNMENT WITHIN A RELATIONSHIP ∿

- Do I take time to reflect quietly upon the development of this relationship and its significance in my life?
- Would some solitude help me to understand better God's call in this relationship?
- Have we had some quality time to be together away from intense activity and groups?

DISCERNMENT WITHIN A GROUP ∿

- How comfortable are we with moments of silence during our time together?

A DISCERNING RELATIONSHIP WITH THE WORLD ∿

- What practices have I learned from other religious traditions that help me become still?
- What types of visual images foster stillness in me?
- Do I allow times of stillness to influence my efforts to help transform a violent society?

Vatican Council II

"When they [the people] are drawn to think about their real selves they turn to those deep recesses of their being where God who probes the heart awaits them, and where they themselves decide their own destiny in the sight of God" (Pastoral Constitution on the Church in the Modern World, GS 14, 177).

Openness

Openness to the ordinary and extraordinary action of God within relationships contributes to our readiness to become more discerning and to accept the conclusion reached in discernment. Relationships depend upon openness.

Ignatian Insights

"After the pilgrim [Ignatius] realized that it was God's will that he not stay in Jerusalem, he continually pondered within himself what he ought to do; and eventually he was rather inclined to study for some time so he would be able to help souls" (*Autobiography*, 50).

"The person . . . will benefit greatly . . . by offering all their desires and freedom to him so that His Divine Majesty can make use of their persons and of all they possess in whatsoever way is in accord with his most holy will" (*Spiritual Exercises*, 5).

Scripture

"Then Elisha prayed: 'O LORD, please open his eyes that he may see.' And the LORD opened the eyes of the servant, and he saw . . ." (2 Kings 6:17).

"Open my eyes, so that I may behold wondrous things . . ." (Psalm 119:18).

"Listen! I am standing at the door, knocking; if you hear my voice and open the door, I will come in to you and eat with you, and you with me" (Revelation 3:20).

"Let anyone who has an ear listen to what the Spirit is saying to the churches" (Revelation 2:29).

Grace

To be open to the multiple ways in which God speaks to me each day in the context of relationships.

"Be like those who are waiting for their master to return from the wedding banquet, so that they may open the door for him as soon as he comes and knocks" (Luke 12:36).

Reflection Questions

CONSIDERATIONS FOR PRAYER

- Am I open to being led to a new place in my relationship with God?
- How does my physical and emotional condition affect my openness to other people and to God's action in and through them?

DISCERNMENT WITHIN A RELATIONSHIP

- How open am I to new relationships or to changes in ongoing relationships?
- What helps me to allow time and space for the consideration of new ideas and options?

DISCERNMENT WITHIN A GROUP

- Are we open to being joined by new people?
- Are we open to the possibility that God may lead us to some different ways of interacting as a group?

A DISCERNING RELATIONSHIP WITH THE WORLD

- How does information about global crises challenge my attitudes and opinions?
- What helps me to maintain a balanced openness when being influenced by many diverse opinions?

Further Resources

Psalm 51:51

Psalm 119:18

Proverbs 9:9

Mark 8:15

Luke 12:36

Vatican Council II

"Those also have a claim on our respect and charity who think and act differently from us in social, political and religious matters. In fact the more deeply, through kindness and love, we come to understand their ways of thinking, the more easily will we be able to enter into dialogue with them" (GS 28, 193).

"People look to their different religions for an answer to the unsolved riddles of human existence. The problems that weigh heavily on peoples' hearts are the same today as in ages past. What is humanity? What is the meaning and purpose of life? What is upright behavior. . . . Where does suffering originate, and what end does it serve? How can genuine happiness be found? What happens at death. . . . And finally, what is the ultimate mystery, beyond human explanation, which embraces our entire existence, from which we take our origin and toward which we tend?" (Declaration on the Relation of the Church to Non-Christian Religions, NA 1, 569–570).

Honesty

The truth of our existence is found in who we are before a loving and merciful God. That reality grounds honesty with God, with ourselves, and with others. Authentic relationships require honesty, directness, and integrity. Commitment to honesty is a strength and an absolute requisite for discernment of God's will in any situation.

Ignatian Insights

"Up to the age of twenty-six he was a man given to the follies of the world; and what he enjoyed most was exercise with arms, having a great and foolish desire to win fame" (*Autobiography*, 1).

". . . the enemy acts like a false lover, insofar as he tries to remain secret and undetected. . . . In a similar manner, when the enemy of human nature turns his wiles and persuasions upon an upright person, he intends and desires them to be received and kept in secrecy. But when the person reveals them to his or her good confessor or some other spiritual person who understands the enemy's deceits and malice, he is grievously disappointed. For he quickly sees that he cannot succeed in the malicious project he began, because his manifest deceptions have been detected" (*Spiritual Exercises*, 326).

"Imagine Christ our Lord suspended on the cross before you, and converse with him in a colloquy. . . . In a similar way, reflect on yourself and ask: What have I done for Christ? What am I doing for Christ? What ought I to do for Christ?" (*Spiritual Exercises*, 53).

Grace

To be willing to pay the price for being honest with myself, with God, and with others.

Scripture [399]

"Birds roost with their own kind, so honesty comes home to those who practice it" (Sirach 27:9).

"How forceful are honest words!" (Job 6:25).

". . . hear the word, hold it fast in an honest and good heart, and bear fruit with patient endurance" (Luke 8:15).

"So they watched him and sent spies who pretended to be honest, in order to trap him by what he said, so as to hand him over to the jurisdiction and authority of the governor" (Luke 20:20).

"The [Samaritan] woman said to him, 'Sir, give me this water, so that I may never be thirsty or have to keep coming here to draw water.' Jesus said to her, 'Go, call your husband, and come back.' The woman answered him, 'I have no husband.' Jesus answered her, 'You are right in saying, "I have no husband"; for you have had five husbands, and the one you have now is not your husband. What you have said is true!'" (John 4:15–18).

"When he had finished speaking, he said to Simon, 'Put out into the deep water and let down your nets for a catch.' Simon answered, 'Master, we have worked all night long but have caught nothing. Yet if you say so, I will let down the nets.' When they had done this, they caught so many fish that their nets were beginning to break. So they signaled their partners in the other boat to come to help them. And they came and filled both boats, so that they began to sink. When Simon Peter saw it, he fell at Jesus' knees, saying, 'Go away from me, Lord, for I am a sinful man!'" (Luke 5:4–8).

Further Resources

Luke 4:16–21, 24–30

John 1:19–23, 29–31, 34

Luke 7:18–23

Luke 8:43–48

John 14:5–9

Spiritual Exercises 6—AA13, 421

Reflection Questions

CONSIDERATIONS FOR PRAYER

- When did I learn the importance of being honest?
- Have I discovered that reflective prayer in God's presence can be a way in which I address any fears that keep me from being honest?
- What challenges have resulted from my being honest with myself or others?
- How has honesty with God matured my relationship with God?

DISCERNMENT WITHIN A RELATIONSHIP

- Is our relationship characterized by mutual honesty and directness?
- How open am I to a fuller understanding of myself that may result from another's honesty with me?
- What constructive ways of giving feedback to each other have we learned in our relationship?
- What comfort do I experience when I can count on another's honesty with me?

DISCERNMENT WITHIN A GROUP

- Have we learned to put aside our roles and personae so that we can engage in honest conversation?
- Do we receive one another's honesty with respect and reverence?
- How do we deal with our fears of interacting honestly within the group or with people outside the group?

- Have I learned to be critically reflective of the actions of public figures, organizations, and the media as I search for truth about local, national, and world situations?

- Do I use my access to systems and any influence I have within them to present facts honestly and to require that others do the same?

Vatican Council II

"[The laity] should also hold in high esteem professional competence, family and civic sense, and the virtues related to social behavior such as honesty, sense of justice, sincerity, courtesy, moral courage; without them there is no true Christian life" (Decree on the Apostolate of Lay People, AA 4, 409).

"Since it is the Church's job to communicate with the human society in which it lives the bishops should make it their special care to approach people and to initiate and promote dialogue with them. These discussions on religious matters should be marked by clarity of expression as well as by humility and courtesy, so that truth may be combined with charity, and understanding with love. The discussions should likewise be characterized by due prudence allied, however, to confidence. This, by encouraging friendship, is conducive to a union of minds" (Decree on the Pastoral Office of Bishops in the Church, CD 13, 290).

Awareness

A discerning faith invites us to be aware of both the ordinary and the unexpected ways in which God's desires are revealed. Awareness develops as we notice the sometimes subtle changes in ourselves and in our efforts to be discerning when reverencing our feelings and experiences. Without bringing this awareness to relationships, we can miss the call of grace.

Ignatian Insights

"But soon after the temptation [being troubled at the prospect of a life of hardships] . . . he began to have great changes in his soul. Sometimes he felt so out of sorts that he found no relish in saying prayers nor in hearing Mass nor in any other devotion he might practice. At other times quite the opposite of this came over him so suddenly that he seemed to have thrown off sadness and desolation just as one snatches a cape from another's shoulders. Now he started getting perturbed by the changes that he had never experienced before, and he said to himself, 'What new life is this that we are now beginning?'" (*Autobiography*, 21).

"Rules for the Discernment of Spirits: Rules to aid us toward perceiving and then understanding, at least to some extent, the various motions which are caused in the soul: the good motions that they may be received and the bad that they may be rejected" (*Spiritual Exercises*, 313).

Scripture

"She came up behind him and touched the fringe of his clothes, and immediately her hemorrhage stopped. Jesus then asked, 'Who touched me?' When all denied it,

Grace

To become increasingly conscious of my interior thoughts and feelings in the midst of relationships.

Peter said, 'Master, the crowds surround you and press in on you.' But Jesus said, 'Someone touched me; for I noticed that power has gone out from me'" (Luke 8:44–46).

"As he came near and saw the city, he wept over it, saying, 'If you, even you, had only recognized on this day the things that make for peace! But now they are hidden from your eyes'" (Luke 19:41–42).

"But Jesus on his part . . . knew what was in everyone"(John 2:24–25).

Reflection Questions

CONSIDERATIONS FOR PRAYER

- What prayer form has helped me to become aware of my feelings?
- Do I recognize the importance of distinguishing thoughts from feelings?
- How have my experiences shaped the way I deal with feelings?
- What grace do I need so that I can accept my feelings with peace?
- What thoughts and feelings can block my consciousness of my desires?

DISCERNMENT WITHIN A RELATIONSHIP

- What hopes do I have for growing in discernment in this relationship?
- What practices help me to clarify my own thoughts and feelings about another person?
- Am I aware of the thought patterns or particular feelings that can predominate in my ways of relating to others?
- Am I aware of any destructive patterns in the relationship?

Further Resources

Luke 10:21
Spiritual Exercises 17
GS 91, 279

DISCERNMENT WITHIN A GROUP ∿

- What steps have we taken to ensure that the thoughts and feelings of each person in the group will be met with respect?

- How does the group respect boundaries and confidentiality?

A DISCERNING RELATIONSHIP WITH THE WORLD ∿

- Am I aware of changes in my thoughts and feelings about the earth and my role in sustaining it?

- How do I integrate my understanding of justice into my thoughts and feelings about current world events?

- Am I aware of my need to be more knowledgeable about and sensitive to other cultures?

Vatican Council II

". . . A huge proportion of the people of the world is plagued by hunger and extreme need while countless numbers are totally illiterate. At no time have people had such a keen sense of freedom, only to be faced by new forms of social and psychological slavery. . . . We have not yet seen the last of bitter political, social, and economic hostility, and racial and ideological antagonism, nor are we free from the specter of a war of total destruction" (GS 4, 166).

"Many, it is true, fail to see the dramatic nature of this state of affairs in all its clarity for their vision is in fact blurred by materialism, or they are prevented from even thinking about it by the wretchedness of their plight" (GS 10, 171).

Recognition of My Religious Experience

One of God's gifts is the ability to recognize God's action and presence within us. Discernment invites us to deepen our sensitivity to that mysterious experience. While this experience may occur with or through other people, God is free to touch us in other ways that surprise us.

Ignatian Insights

"One day, a few miles before reaching Rome, he (Ignatius) was at prayer in a church and experienced such a change in his soul and saw so clearly that God the Father placed him with Christ his Son that he would not dare doubt it—that God the Father had placed him with his Son" (*Autobiography*, 96).

"God treated him at this time just as a schoolmaster treats a child whom he is teaching. Whether this was because of his lack of education and of brains, or because he had no one to teach him, or because of the strong desire God himself had given him to serve him, he believed without doubt and has always believed that God treated him in this way. Indeed if he were to doubt this, he would think he offended his Divine Majesty" (*Autobiography*, 27).

"When a person is seeking God's will, it is more appropriate and far better that the Creator and Lord himself should communicate himself to the devout soul, embracing it in love and praise, and disposing it for the way which will enable the soul to serve him better in the future" (*Spiritual Exercises*, 15).

Grace

To remember those times in my life when I experienced God in a way that left no doubt within me.

Further Resources

Ezekiel 37:14

Job 32:8

John 10:25, 37–38

Spiritual Exercises 330

LG 11, 16

Scripture

"Moses was keeping the flock of his father-in-law Jethro, the priest of Midian; he led his flock beyond the wilderness, and came to Horeb, the mountain of God. There the angel of the LORD appeared to him in a flame of fire out of a bush; he looked, and the bush was blazing, yet it was not consumed. Then Moses said, 'I must turn aside and look at this great sight, and see why the bush is not burned up.' When the LORD saw that he had turned aside to see, God called to him out of the bush, "Moses, Moses!' And he said, 'Here I am.' Then he said, 'Come no closer! Remove the sandals from your feet, for the place on which you are standing is holy ground'" (Exodus 3:1–5).

"Therefore I prayed, and understanding was given me; I called on God, and the spirit of wisdom came to me" (Wisdom 7:7).

"And when Jesus had been baptized, just as he came up from the water, suddenly the heavens were opened to him and he saw the Spirit of God descending like a dove and alighting on him. And a voice from heaven said, 'This is my Son, the Beloved, with whom I am well pleased.' Then Jesus was led up by the Spirit into the wilderness to be tempted by the devil" (Matthew 3:16–17; 4:1).

"Do you know that you are God's temple and that God's Spirit dwells in you?" (1 Corinthians 3:16).

Reflection Questions

CONSIDERATIONS FOR PRAYER

- What do I notice when I bring my ordinary experience to God in prayer?
- When did I begin to be aware that I have experiences of God? What was my initial reaction to that gift?

- Do I respect the complex nature of religious experience? Have I learned to be respectful and discerning about my religious experience?

- What patterns in my thoughts and emotions accompany my being touched by God?

DISCERNMENT WITHIN A RELATIONSHIP ∿

- Do I experience the presence and action of God in the midst of relationships? What does this tell me about the relationships?

- Have I ever walked away from the awareness that resulted from my experience of God? What did it feel like to walk away from that awareness?

DISCERNMENT WITHIN A GROUP ∿

- What difference does opening ourselves to an experience of God make to our interactions and decision making?

A DISCERNING RELATIONSHIP WITH THE WORLD ∿

- How have literature, the sciences, and the mysteries of creation helped me to reverence the many diverse ways in which I can experience the transcendent?

- How does respect for the religious experience of people of various faith traditions contribute to my relationships with them?

Vatican Council II

"When we look on the lives of those women and men who have faithfully followed Christ we are inspired anew to seek the city which is to come, while at the same time we are taught about the safest path by which, through a changing world and in keeping with each one's state of life and condition, we will be able to arrive at perfect union with Christ, which is holiness" (Dogmatic Constitution on the Church, 50, 76).

THE DISCERNMENT PROCESS:
Prayer and Examen

Prayer and Examen are essential practices for discernment.

The Spirit guides all of our prayer. Our challenge is to become attuned to the delicate invitations and gifts of the Spirit when we pray and as we live in relationships and in service.

The Spirit will roam freely within our feelings as well as in our thoughts, so a growing attentiveness to both thoughts and feelings is essential. Discernment, which is a faith process, draws insight and awareness of the diverse spirits and movements within our hearts from our times of prayer, especially from the Examen prayer.

A daily time of quiet, personal reflective prayer allows us to open to the action of the Spirit who invites, leads, prompts, cajoles, inspires, delights, urges, challenges, clarifies, and reassures us in our search for God's gracious will. The gospels nourish our loving relationship with Jesus which is a fundamental source of discerning God's will in our lives. Being attuned to God in prayer and activity is foundational to noticing the movements of various spirits within us. Noticing those movements is at the core of the discernment process. Gradually we become aware of any bias, injustice, or lack of interior freedom which is influencing us. A heart that has gradually become attuned to God in prayer will be able to be attuned to God in activity—to be contemplative in the midst of action.

By the term "Spiritual Exercises" we mean every method of examination of conscience, meditation, contemplation, vocal, or mental prayer, and other spiritual activities . . . the name given to any means of preparing and disposing our soul to rid itself of all disordered affections and then, after their removal, of seeking and finding God's will in the ordering of our life for the salvation of our soul (*Spiritual Exercises*, 1).

The Examen prayer, one of the "spiritual exercises" that Ignatius presents in the *Spiritual Exercises*, becomes for us a time of daily discernment. The Examen is truly meant to be a prayer experience. Beginning with a prayer to the Holy Spirit begging for light and guidance, we reflect on the events of the day as part of our relationship with God. With the help of the Spirit, we give a daily prayerful consideration to our day's experience, noting the many gifts of the day. Once conscious of God's gifts to us, we are able to remember our responses and reactions to the gifts and, thus, to examine with more care and wisdom what a given day really held for us. This prayer of Examen offers us a way of noting patterns of grace as well as our acceptance or resistance to God's action. The prayer concludes with our asking for God's forgiveness for any poor response and for God's help in the day ahead.

Taken together, prayer and Examen are two human activities through which we express our desire to discover God's mysterious ways in our minds, hearts, spirits, and bodies as well as in the events and relationships of our lives. They are the steady context within which the discernment process unfolds. It is important to share one's experience of prayer and Examen during a time of discernment with one's spiritual director.

> If the one giving the Exercises sees that the [person] is proceeding with consolation and great fervor, he or she should warn the person not to make some promise or vow which is unconsidered or hasty. The more unstable the director sees the [person] to be, the more earnest should be the forewarning and caution . . . one ought to bestow much thought on the strength and suitability of each person, and on the helps or hindrances one is likely to meet with in carrying out what one wishes to promise (*Spiritual Exercises*, 14).

Reflection Questions

- How has my prayer been enriched and focused by reflection on my daily experience?
- What are my hopes for growing as a discerning person by adding daily personal prayer and the Examen prayer to my daily routine?
- What new trust in my capacity to experience God's presence and action is growing within me?
- How are prayer and the Examen helping me to discover my true and developing identity?
- What is my response to God's call to me to be more just in my daily life?
- How does viewing my day through the lens of justice/injustice make me aware of God's invitation to me?

Moment *of* Identity

Mary's Story

In the sixth month the angel Gabriel was sent by God to a town in Galilee called Nazareth, to a virgin engaged to a man whose name was Joseph, of the house of David. The virgin's name was Mary.

~Luke 1:26–27

The Emmaus Story

Jesus himself came near and went with them, but their eyes were kept from recognizing him. And he said to them, "What are you discussing with each other while you walk along?" They stood still, looking sad.

~Luke 24:15–17

Early in a relationship—with God or with another—one shares one's identity and self-understanding. Since one's identity and self-understanding are such fundamental touchstones in discernment, this moment is a time to grow in the ability to listen with care to oneself, others, and God. I need to be attentive to the varied interior movements of my own mind, heart, body, and spirit. These qualities help me to become more perceptive as I articulate my faith experience. In turn, this will enable me to clarify and accept my growing sense of who I am before God.

Listening

Listening plays an important role in discernment. Initially, we are invited to a careful listening to our own interiority. As we become more adept at attending to our own thoughts, feelings, and intuitions, we grow in sensitivity and fidelity to our true identity. Attentive listening to God's Word in scripture and in life helps us move to the freedom and objectivity needed for discernment.

Ignatian Insights

"Ever since Manresa the pilgrim had the habit when he ate with anyone, never to speak at table, except to answer briefly: but he listened to what was said and noted some things which he took as the occasion to speak about God, and when the meal was finished, he did so" (*Autobiography*, 42).

"I will listen to what the persons on the face of the earth are saying; that is, how they speak with one another, swear and blaspheme, and so on. Likewise, I will hear what the Divine Persons are saying, that is, 'Let us work the redemption of the human race,' and so forth. Then I will listen to what the angel and Our Lady are saying. Afterwards I will reflect on this, to draw profit from their words" (*Spiritual Exercises*, 107).

Scripture

"Therefore, as the Holy Spirit says, 'Today, if you hear his voice, do not harden your hearts'" (Hebrews 3:7–8).

"Then those who revered the LORD spoke with one another. The LORD took note and listened, and a book of remembrance was written before him of those who

Grace

To listen with care to my interior feelings, thoughts, intuitions, and questions, all of which can carry God's action in my life.

revered the LORD and thought on his name. 'They shall be mine', says the LORD . . . 'my special possession . . .'" (Malachi 3:16–17).

"But just when he had resolved to do this, an angel of the Lord appeared to him in a dream and said, 'Joseph, son of David, do not be afraid to take Mary as your wife, for the child conceived in her is from the Holy Spirit'" (Matthew 1:20).

"Then a cloud overshadowed them, and from the cloud there came a voice, 'This is my Son, the Beloved; listen to him!'" (Mark 9:7).

"'Some fell into good soil, and when it grew, it produced a hundredfold.' As he said this, he called out, 'Let anyone with ears to hear listen!'" (Luke 8:8).

Reflection Questions

CONSIDERATIONS FOR PRAYER

- When have I felt listened to with attentiveness? What response did that call forth from me?

- Am I learning to listen to my own interiority? What indicates that I am listening in prayer?

- Am I growing in respect for the thoughts, feelings, questions, and intuitions that are part of my interiority?

- What do I discover when I pay attention to my interior reactions and responses?

- Do I believe that God listens to me?

DISCERNMENT WITHIN A RELATIONSHIP

- What challenges do I experience in listening to another?

- What are our shared life experiences teaching me?

Further Resources

Revelation 3:20

Luke 8:16–18

DISCERNMENT WITHIN A GROUP ⁓

- As I listen to diverse views, what is stirred within me?
- How do I stay open and attentive?

A DISCERNING RELATIONSHIP WITH THE WORLD ⁓

- What do I do with the feelings that get stirred in me as I listen to the descriptions of the suffering of people?

Vatican Council II

"Deep within their consciences men and women discover a law which they have not laid upon themselves and which they must obey. . . . For they have in their hearts a law inscribed by God. Their dignity rests in observing this law, and by it they will be judged. Their conscience is people's most secret core and their sanctuary. There they are alone with God whose voice echoes in their depths" (GS 16, 178).

"[Christ] is present in his word since it is he himself who speaks when the holy scriptures are read in church. Lastly, he is present when the church prays and sings, for he has promised 'where two or three are gathered together in my name there am I in the midst of them' (Mt 18:20)" (The Constitution on the Sacred Liturgy, SC 7, 121).

Attentiveness

. . . .

The practice of attentiveness prepares us to notice the delicate action of God within our thoughts, feelings, and life experiences. Reverent attentiveness to the pattern of specific thoughts and feelings often reveals their significance and meaning within our personal history. Attentiveness makes room for a discernment and interpretation of thoughts and feelings that lead us forward in fidelity to our personal identity.

Ignatian Insights

"I should notice and dwell on those points where I felt greater consolation or desolation, or had a greater spiritual experience" (*Spiritual Exercises*, 62).

"Reading the life of our Lord and of the saints, he stopped to think, reasoning within himself: 'What if I should do this which Saint Francis did, and this which Saint Dominic did?' Thus he pondered over many things that he found good . . . . This succession of such diverse thoughts lasted for quite some time and he always dwelt at length upon the thoughts that turned up . . . until he tired of it and put it aside and turned to other matters" (*Autobiography*, 7).

"However, the spiritual person to whom God gives this consolation ought to examine that experience with great vigilance and attention. One should distinguish the time when the consolation itself was present from the time after it, in which the soul remains still warm and favored with the gifts and aftereffects of the consolation which has itself passed away. For often during this later period we ourselves act either through our own reasoning which springs from our own habits and the conclusions we draw from our own concepts and judgments, or through the influence of either a good or an evil spirit. In this way we form various projects and convictions which are

Grace

To grow in my attentiveness to the dynamic interplay of my thoughts, feelings, and desires.

not coming immediately from God our Lord. Hence these need to be very carefully examined before they are fully accepted or carried into effect" (*Spiritual Exercises*, Rules for Discernment, 336).

Scripture

"Elijah said to Ahab, 'Go up, eat and drink; for there is a sound of rushing rain.' So Ahab went up to eat and to drink. Elijah went up to the top of Carmel; there he bowed himself down upon the earth and put his face between his knees. He said to his servant, 'Go up now, look toward the sea.' He went up and looked, and said, 'There is nothing.' Then he said, 'Go again seven times.' At the seventh time he said, 'Look, a little cloud no bigger than a person's hand is rising out of the sea.' . . . In a little while the heavens grew black with clouds and wind; there was a heavy rain" (1 Kings 18:41–45).

"Jacob's well was there, and Jesus, tired out by his journey, was sitting by the well. It was about noon. A Samaritan woman came to draw water, and Jesus said to her, 'Give me a drink.' . . . The Samaritan woman said to him, 'How is it that you, a Jew, ask a drink of me, a woman of Samaria?' . . . Jesus answered her, 'If you knew the gift of God, and who it is that is saying to you, "Give me a drink," you would have asked him, and he would have given you living water.' The woman said to him, 'Sir, you have no bucket, and the well is deep. Where do you get that living water?'" (John 4:6–11).

"He said to him the third time, 'Simon son of John, do you love me?' Peter felt hurt because he said to him the third time, 'Do you love me?' And he said to him, 'Lord, you know everything; you know that I love you.' Jesus said to him, 'Feed my sheep'" (John 21:17).

Further Resources

Proverbs 16:20

Hebrews 4:12

Reflection Questions

CONSIDERATIONS FOR PRAYER

- What tends to block my attentiveness to God in prayer?
- What types of feelings do I generally attend to with ease? What types of feelings do I generally prefer to ignore or deny?
- Under what conditions am I most creative in my thought?
- What experiences have I had of drawing upon intuition as a way of knowing something?
- Am I conscious of, but not limited to, the sequences of logical thought?

DISCERNMENT WITHIN A RELATIONSHIP

- Throughout my life, what have relationships taught me about reverencing human experience?
- In my relationships, have I experienced congruence between the words spoken and accompanying behavior? What helps me to grow in that kind of congruence and integrity?

DISCERNMENT WITHIN A GROUP

- Are we becoming more attentive to the mysterious combination of gifts that each person brings to the group?

A DISCERNING RELATIONSHIP WITH THE WORLD

- Am I using justice as a criterion for deciding to which world issues I will give my attention?
- Have I made attention to the cry of the earth a part of my daily faith response?

Vatican Council II

"Since in our days women are taking an increasingly active share in the entire life of society, it is very important that their participation in the various sectors of the church's apostolate should likewise develop" (AA 9, 416).

"The genius of humankind, especially in our times, has produced marvelous technical inventions from creation, with God's help. Mother church is particularly interested in those which directly touch the human spirit and which have opened up new avenues of easy communication of all kinds of news, ideas, and directives. Chief among them are those means of communication which of their nature can reach and influence not just single individuals but the very masses and even the whole of human society. These are the press, the cinema, radio, television and others of like nature. These can rightly be called the means of social communication" (Decree on the Media of Communication, IM 1, p. 539).

Articulation of My Faith Experience

The wondrous activity of God is to be found in experiences, those that may seem important and even those that may seem trivial. Their significance is found in God's presence to us in the experience. As we become more discerning, opportunities to share our faith experience as well as our growing awareness of the interior movements during an experience can help us to interpret it.

Ignatian Insights

"Similarly the enemy acts like a false lover, insofar as he tries to remain secret and undetected. For such a scoundrel, speaking with evil intent and trying to seduce the daughter of a good father or the wife of a good husband, wants his words and solicitations to remain secret. But he is deeply displeased when the daughter reveals his deceitful words and evil design to her father, or the wife to her husband. For he easily infers that he cannot succeed in the design he began.

"In a similar manner, when the enemy of human nature turns his wiles and persuasions upon an upright person, he intends and desires them to be received and kept in secrecy. But when the person reveals them to his or her good confessor or some other spiritual person who understands the enemy's deceits and malice, he is grievously disappointed. For he quickly sees that he cannot succeed in the malicious project he began, because his manifest deceptions have been detected" (*Spiritual Exercises*, Rules for Discernment, 326).

Grace

To grow in the vulnerability needed as I articulate my faith experience to others.

Scripture

"Mary took a pound of costly perfume made of pure nard, anointed Jesus' feet, and wiped them with her hair. The house was filled with the fragrance of the perfume" (John 12:3).

"Now when Jesus came into the district of Caesarea Philippi, he asked his disciples, 'Who do people say that the Son of Man is?' And they said, 'Some say John the Baptist, but others Elijah, and still others Jeremiah or one of the prophets.' He said to them, 'But who do you say that I am?' Simon Peter answered, 'You are the Messiah, the Son of the living God.' And Jesus answered him, 'Blessed are you, Simon son of Jonah! For flesh and blood has not revealed this to you, but my Father in heaven'" (Matthew 16:13–17).

"[Mary] turned around and saw Jesus standing there, but she did not know that it was Jesus. Jesus said to her, 'Woman, why are you weeping? Whom are you looking for?' Supposing him to be the gardener, she said to him, 'Sir, if you have carried him away, tell me where you have laid him, and I will take him away.' Jesus said to her, 'Mary!' She turned and said to him in Hebrew, 'Rabbouni!' (which means Teacher). . . . Mary Magdalene went and announced to the disciples, 'I have seen the Lord'; and she told them that he had said these things to her" (John 20:14–18).

Reflection Questions

CONSIDERATIONS FOR PRAYER

- Who has encouraged me to trust and articulate my experience? How have they done that?

- What do I notice when I share my experience of faith or prayer with another?

- Am I developing a vocabulary to articulate my experience, especially my experience of the presence and action of God?

- Have I noticed a growing confidence about my relationship with God as a result of opportunities to share it with others?

- Do I sometimes refrain from sharing my faith experience with others? Why can this be a good thing to do?

DISCERNMENT WITHIN A RELATIONSHIP ∼

- Are my significant relationships ones in which I feel free to articulate my faith perspective about public as well as personal topics?

DISCERNMENT WITHIN A GROUP ∼

- How does articulating our faith experiences with each other affect our interactions as a group?

- How confident am I in articulating my faith perspective about both personal and public events?

- What practical steps can I take to grow in that confidence?

A DISCERNING RELATIONSHIP WITH THE WORLD ∼

- What is the challenge for me of including my faith perspective in conversations about controversial world events?

- What reading or other forms of inquiry can help me to increase my understanding of the Christian perspective on topics such as those developed in Catholic social teaching?

Vatican Council II

"The tradition that comes from the apostles makes progress in the church, with the help of the holy Spirit. There is a growth in insight into the realities and words that are being passed on. This comes about through the contemplation and study of believers who ponder these things in their hearts (see Lk 2:19 and 51). It comes from the intimate sense of spiritual realities which they experience" (Dogmatic Constitution on Divine Revelation, DV 8, 102).

"With the help of the Holy Spirit, it is the task of the whole people of God, particularly of its pastors and theologians, to listen to and distinguish the many voices of our times and to interpret them in the light of God's word, in order that the revealed truth may be more deeply penetrated, better understood, and more suitably presented" (GS 44, 215).

Growing Acceptance of My Identity

Discernment begins with our personal identity before God. Discernment continuously refines and confirms this identity. As our consciousness of the significance of our baptismal identity develops, that identity in Christ offers practical criteria for our self-image, happiness, and success. God continually calls us to an acceptance of our personal identity. Discernment helps this ongoing process.

Ignatian Insights

"He said . . . he had always grown in devotion, that is, ease in finding God; and now more than ever in his whole life. Every time, any hour, that he wished to find God, he found him. And even now he often had visions, especially those mentioned above in which he saw Christ as the sun. This often happened while he was engaged in important matters, and that gave him confirmation" (*Autobiography*, 99).

"The Second Time (for making a sound and good election) is present when sufficient clarity and knowledge are received from the experience of consolations and desolations, and from experience in the discernment of various spirits" (*Spiritual Exercises*, 176).

"For everyone ought to reflect that in all spiritual matters, the more one divests oneself of self-love, self-will, and self-interests, the more progress one will make" (*Spiritual Exercises*, 189).

Grace

To accept more graciously my identity, which has developed from my experiences and choices.

Scripture

"The spirit of God has made me, and the breath of the Almighty gives me life" (Job 33:4).

"A new heart I will give you, and a new spirit I will put within you; and I will remove from your body the heart of stone and give you a heart of flesh" (Ezekiel 36:26).

"After three days they found him in the temple, sitting among the teachers, listening to them and asking them questions. And all who heard him were amazed at his understanding and his answers. When his parents saw him they were astonished; and his mother said to him, 'Child, why have you treated us like this? Look, your father and I have been searching for you in great anxiety.' He said to them, 'Why were you searching for me? Did you not know that I must be in my Father's house?' But they did not understand what he said to them. Then he went down with them and came to Nazareth, and was obedient to them. His mother treasured all things in her heart. And Jesus increased in wisdom and in years, and in divine and human favor" (Luke 2:46–52).

"And all of us, with unveiled faces, seeing the glory of the Lord as though reflected in a mirror, are being transformed into the same image from one degree of glory to another; for this comes from the Lord, the Spirit" (2 Corinthians 3:18).

Reflection Questions

CONSIDERATIONS FOR PRAYER

- What aspect of my personal identity offers a continual challenge to my honest self-acceptance?

Further Resources

Matthew 3:16–17

Romans 8:5, 14–17

LG 36, 54–55

GS 61, 237

- What helps me to guard against discouragement regarding that aspect of my identity?
- What choices—both good and poor choices—have played a significant part in forming the person I have become?
- Are my priorities consistent with my current life stage and do I review them from time to time?
- What sufferings have played a significant part in forming my personal identity?

DISCERNMENT WITHIN A RELATIONSHIP

- How are my relationships affecting my personal identity?
- Do my relationships allow me to change and grow?
- Do I offer others an affirmation of their growing identity?
- How am I balancing the demands of time made by my relationships?

DISCERNMENT WITHIN A GROUP

- How would I characterize the identity of this group?
- Are the defining boundaries of this group flexible enough to keep us open to God's invitation to become more faithful disciples of Christ?

A DISCERNING RELATIONSHIP WITH THE WORLD

- What organizations and institutions have influenced me significantly as I have moved through my life? In what ways do they still influence my adult identity?
- How do I limit the impact on my identity of cultural trends that reveal themselves to be destructive of, or alien to, my adult Christian identity?

Vatican Council II

"The dichotomy affecting the modern world is, in fact, a symptom of the deeper dichotomy that is rooted in humanity itself. It is the meeting point of many conflicting forces. As created beings, people are subject to many limitations, but they feel unlimited in their desires and their sense of being destined for a higher life. They feel the pull of many attractions and are compelled to choose between them and reject some among them. Worse still, feeble and sinful as they are, they often do the very thing they hate and do not do what they want. And so they feel themselves divided, and the result is a host of discords in social life. . . . Nonetheless, in the face of modern developments there is a growing body of people who are asking the most fundamental of all questions or are glimpsing them with a keener insight: What is humanity? What is the meaning of suffering, evil, death, which have not been eliminated by all this progress? What is the purpose of these achievements, purchased at so high a price? What can people contribute to society? What can they expect from it? What happens after this earthly life is ended?" (GS 10, 171–172).

"Once God is forgotten, the creature itself is left in darkness" (GS 36, 202).

THE DISCERNMENT PROCESS:
Consolation and Desolation

Consolation and desolation are interior movements of the heart attended to within the discernment process.

L ike background music at our favorite restaurant, consolation and desolation can be part of our experience without our even noticing them. They are often carried within our emotions and feelings. When finally noticed, they give new richness and depth to our experience. For some, the first awareness of consolation and desolation occurs as one becomes aware of what seem to be strong emotions or even mood swings. Befriending those various feelings by noticing, accepting, and reverencing them carries us a long way toward becoming more attuned to our interior world. A reflective person notices changes in affectivity as a day unfolds and gradually recognizes that the actual meaning of the change may be different from what was initially perceived.

With practice, in a variety of circumstances, one notices oneself more attuned to the interior changes which occur. We discover that what is happening is more than just "having a good or bad day." Often we find within our hearts a mixture of both consolation and desolation as we act and respond in any situation. Our feelings can range from gratitude, interior harmony, and tears of joy to turmoil, futility, restlessness, and agitation. Part of the work of discernment is to sort out this mixture, giving name and interpretation to each of the different elements. Ignatius learned that different expressions of consolation seem to cluster together, yielding a recognizable pattern. Expressions of desolation also tend to cluster, yielding a pattern which is opposite to the pattern of consolation.

Yet Ignatius recognized that there was this difference.

When he was thinking of those things of the world, he took much delight in them, but afterwards, when he was tired and put them aside, he found himself dry and dissatisfied. But when he thought of going to Jerusalem, not only was he consoled when he had these thoughts but even after putting them aside he remained satisfied and joyful (*Autobiography*, 8).

Thus, a new dimension is added to our self-knowledge as we discover the unique ways in which we experience both consolation and desolation. This is how Ignatius describes these movements:

About spiritual consolation: By [this kind of] consolation I mean that which occurs when some interior motion is caused within the soul through which it comes to be inflamed with love of its Creator and Lord. As a result it can love no

59

created thing on the face of the earth in itself, but only in the Creator of them all.

Similarly, this consolation is experienced when the soul sheds tears which move it to love for its Lord—whether they are tears of grief for its own sins, or about the Passion of Christ our Lord, or about other matters directly ordered to his service and praise.

Finally, under the word consolation I include every increase in hope, faith, and charity, and every interior joy which calls and attracts one toward heavenly things and to the salvation of one's soul, by bringing it tranquility and peace in its Creator and Lord" (*Spiritual Exercises*, Rules for Discernment, 316).

About spiritual desolation: By [this kind of] desolation I mean everything which is the contrary of what was described in the Third Rule; for example, obtuseness of soul, turmoil within it, an impulsive motion toward low and earthly things, or disquiet from various agitations and temptations. These move one toward lack of faith and leave one without hope and without love. One is completely listless, tepid, and unhappy, and feels separated from our Creator and Lord. For just as consolation is contrary to desolation, so the thoughts which arise from consolation are likewise contrary to those which spring from desolation (*Spiritual Exercises*, Rules for Discernment, 317).

The Rules for Discernment of Spirits of St. Ignatius guide us as we learn what to look for as well as how to reflect upon and respond to the movements of consolation and desolation within our lives. It takes time to appropriate what the terms "consolation" and "desolation" mean and to reflect upon their presence in varying degrees within us.

He did not notice this, however; nor did he stop to ponder the distinction until the time when his eyes were opened a little, and he began to marvel at the difference and to reflect upon it, realizing from experience that some thoughts left him sad and others joyful. Little by little he came to recognize the difference between the spirits that were stirring . . . (*Autobiography*, 8).

Our efforts to grow in awareness and reflection are for the sake of becoming more attuned to the life-giving action of God so that we can cooperate with it as we make our decisions and choices.

While reflection, prayer, and our commitment to a life of Christian virtue dispose us for the gift of discernment, consolation itself is God's gift and grace to us. Not even our best efforts can produce consolation. In time and with experience, we learn that even an experience of desolation can be a gift through which we are drawn closer to God in deeper freedom and humility.

There are three chief causes for the desolation in which we find ourselves. . . . The third is that the desolation is meant to give us a true recognition and understanding, so that we may perceive interiorly that we cannot by ourselves bring on or retain great devotion, intense love, tears, or any other spiritual consolation, but that all these are a gift and grace from God our Lord; and further, to prevent us from building our nest in a house which belongs to Another, by puffing up our minds with pride or vainglory through which we attribute to ourselves the devotion or other features of spiritual consolation (*Spiritual Exercises*, Rules for Discernment, 322).

It is important when the spirit of darkness is at work in our desolation "to act against the desolation and overcome the temptations . . . and in this way become accustomed not merely to resist the enemy but even to defeat him" (*Spiritual Exercises*, 13).

Ignatius, in calling consolation and desolation "spiritual movements," was alerting us to a critical aspect of understanding them and their role in discernment. While often carried within our feelings, consolation and desolation are far different from them. The difference is the result of finding their source in an experience of the action of God. Our Christian faith in God who continues to be incarnate among us through the Spirit points the way to understanding how God can be active within our hearts with the resulting effects of consolation and desolation. Consolation and desolation are experiences that bring us face to face with the mysterious action of God, an action designed to lure us into fuller commitment and surrender to God's ways of justice in our lives and in the world.

But soon after the temptation [being troubled at the prospect of a life of hardships] . . . he began to have great changes in his soul. Sometimes he felt so out of sorts that he found no relish in saying prayers nor in hearing Mass nor in any other devotion he might practice. At other times quite the opposite of this came over him so suddenly that he seemed to have thrown off sadness and desolation just as one snatches a cape from another's shoulders. Now he started getting perturbed by the changes that he had never experienced before, and he said to himself, "What new life is this that we are now beginning" (*Autobiography*, 21).

At this point in the process of *Finding God in Each Moment*, it is important to become familiar with the ways in which you personally experience both consolation and desolation so that you will have, as Ignatius did, access to that information as your discernment unfolds.

CONSIDERATIONS FOR PRAYER ~

- At the end of each time of quiet prayer, spend a few minutes in reflection upon the experience that you just had. Notice where in the prayer you experienced consolation and desolation.

- At the end of each day, notice what consolation and desolation you have experienced throughout the day.

- After some weeks of attending to consolation and desolation in your prayer and daily life, spend some time describing in your own words the ways in which consolation and desolation have been manifested.

DISCERNMENT WITHIN A RELATIONSHIP ~

- In what ways are you the occasion of consolation for each other?

- How are you vulnerable to the movements of desolation in your relationship?

- What have you discovered to be ways of supporting each other when either of you is in consolation or desolation?

- What helps you to recognize that either consolation or desolation is at work in one another?

DISCERNMENT WITHIN A GROUP ~

- Spend a brief time in reflection after each group meeting or gathering so that you can notice the movements of consolation and desolation within yourself during that time together.

- As a result of noticing your experience of consolation and desolation, what self-awareness do you have about your experience in the group?

- Allow time for each member of the group to share, if they wish to do so, their awareness of how they may have experienced consolation and desolation during the time together.

- In light of what you have discovered about the movements of consolation and desolation within the group, are there changes in your group gathering or plans that you want to consider?

A DISCERNING RELATIONSHIP WITH THE WORLD ~

- What seem to be the movements of consolation and desolation within me when I consider the current events of the local, national, and international scenes?

- How can I move against any patterns of desolation stirred in me?

- Am I aware that movements of consolation and desolation can help me to discover patterns of resistance to acting justly?

MOMENT *of* INTIMACY

Annunciation

And he came to her and said, "Greetings, favored one! The Lord is with you."

~LUKE 1:28

Journey to Emmaus

Then one of them, whose name was Cleopas, answered him, "Are you the only stranger in Jerusalem who does not know the things that have taken place there in these days?" He asked them, "What things?" They replied, "The things about Jesus of Nazareth, who was a prophet mighty in deed and word before God and all the people, and how our chief priests and leaders handed him over to be condemned to death and crucified him. But we had hoped that he was the one to redeem Israel. Yes, and besides all this, it is now the third day since these things took place."

~LUKE 24:18–21

While far from being the peak or goal of any Christian relationship, the experience of intimacy in a relationship holds powerful life-giving potential for the way God will incorporate the relationship into God's plan for the world as well as for the individuals in the relationship. This stage of intimacy is often a time of real consolation.

The qualities of a discerning person which emerge and grow in this Moment of Intimacy can bring delight to us, filling us with hope. Growth in these qualities will also be the occasion of questions and challenges. Discernment within this moment will confirm the relationship as God's gift to us. It will also help us to focus on God's call to grow as a person whose relationships are all characterized by desires as well as by human qualities such as reverence, gratitude, trust, prayer, gentleness, and self-knowledge.

Desires

Desires are a favored place for God's action in a person. Revealing both positive and negative energies, our desires may shift and compete for attention as God moves us toward an interior place of harmony rather than of conflict.

Ignatian Insights

"From this lesson he derived not a little light, and he began to think more earnestly about his past life and about the great need he had to do penance for it. At this point the desire to imitate the saints came to him though he gave no thought to particulars, only promising with God's grace to do as they had done. But the one thing he wanted to do was to go to Jerusalem as soon as he recovered, as mentioned above, with as much of disciplines and fasts as a generous spirit, ablaze with God, would want to perform" (*Autobiography*, 9).

"The strong desire God himself had given him to serve him" (*Autobiography*, 27).

"We ought to desire and choose only that which is more conducive to the end for which we are created" (*Spiritual Exercises*, 23).

"The Second Prelude [of a prayer period] is to ask God our Lord for what I want and desire" (*Spiritual Exercises*, 48).

"I will enter upon the contemplation . . . always intent on seeking what I desire" (*Spiritual Exercises*, 76).

Grace

To reverence my human desires as a place where God acts.

Scripture

"As a deer longs for flowing streams, so my soul longs for you, O God. My soul thirsts for God, for the living God. When shall I come and behold the face of God?" (Psalm 42:1–2).

"Create in me a clean heart, O God, and put a new and right spirit within me" (Psalm 51:10).

"Then Jesus said to him, 'What do you want me to do for you?' The blind man said to him, 'My teacher, let me see again.'" (Mark 10:51).

"I say to you, 'Ask, and it will be given you; search, and you will find; knock, and the door will be opened for you. For everyone who asks receives, and everyone who searches finds, and for everyone who knocks, the door will be opened. . . . How much more will the heavenly Father give the Holy Spirit to those who ask him!'" (Luke 11:9–10, 13).

Reflection Questions

CONSIDERATIONS FOR PRAYER

- Am I at ease in praying about my desires?
- When I am still and attentive to God, what desires do I notice surfacing within myself?
- What surprises me about my desires? Am I honest with myself and with others about my desires?
- What desires were prominent at the times of major decisions in my life?
- What is my earliest memory of having desires that led me to action?
- What do I do when I experience the struggle between desires for good and desires that may mask themselves as desires for good?

Further Resources

Matthew 20:20–23

GS 9, 170

DISCERNMENT WITHIN A RELATIONSHIP ∿

- What desires do I have within our relationship at the present time?
- Do I give genuine attention to the desires of others?
- How are we addressing sexual attraction or desire in the relationship?
- What does it mean to be discerning about our shared desires?
- How am I handling the possible conflict of desires within our relationship?

DISCERNMENT WITHIN A GROUP ∿

- As we become more discerning in our interactions, do we notice desires to relate to each other in new ways that may be surfacing?
- How do we work with expressed desires that appear to distract or divert our attention?

A DISCERNING RELATIONSHIP WITH THE WORLD ∿

- Am I conscious of the manipulation of human desire which occurs in contemporary society?
- How do I respond to my desires to better understand people of other cultures?

Vatican Council II

"There appears the dichotomy of a world that is at once powerful and weak, capable of doing what is noble and what is base, disposed to freedom and slavery, progress and decline, amity and hatred. People are becoming conscious that the forces they have unleashed are in their own hands and that it is up to themselves to control them or be enslaved by them. Here lies the modern dilemma. The dichotomy affecting the modern world is, in fact, a symptom of the deeper dichotomy that is rooted in humanity itself. It is the meeting point of many conflicting forces. As created beings, people are subject to many limitations, but they feel unlimited in their desires and their sense of being destined for a higher life. They feel the pull of many attractions and are compelled to choose between them and reject some among them. Worse still, feeble and sinful as they are, they often do the very thing they hate and do not do what they want. And so they feel themselves divided, and the result is a host of discords in social life" (GS 9–10, 171).

Desire to Find God

Fundamental to discernment is the human desire to find God. Discernment focuses this desire upon the discovery of God's will at this time in our life.

Ignatian Insights

"On the way (to Montserrat) something happened to him which it would be well to record, so one may understand how Our Lord dealt with this soul, which was still blind, though greatly desirous of serving him as far as his knowledge went" (*Autobiography*, 14).

"This is to ask God our Lord for what I want and desire. What I ask for should be in accordance with the subject matter. For example, in a contemplation on the Resurrection, I will ask for joy with Christ in joy; in a contemplation on the Passion, I will ask for pain, tears and suffering with Christ suffering" (*Spiritual Exercises*, 48).

"By [this kind of] consolation I mean that which occurs when some interior motion is caused within the soul through which it comes to be inflamed with love of its Creator and Lord. As a result it can love no created thing on the face of the earth in itself, but only in the Creator of them all" 316 (*Spiritual Exercises*, Rules for Discernment).

Scripture

"My soul thirsts for God, for the living God. When shall I come and behold the face of God?" (Psalm 42:2).

"O God, you are my God, I seek you, my soul thirsts for you; my flesh faints for you, as in a dry and weary land where there is no water. . . . Because your steadfast

Grace

To notice and nourish my constant desire to seek God who is present and active in my life.

love is better than life, my lips will praise you. So I will bless you as long as I live; I will lift up my hands and call on your name. My soul is satisfied . . . when I think of you on my bed, and meditate on you in the watches of the night; for you have been my help, and in the shadow of your wings I sing for joy. My soul clings to you; your right hand upholds me" (Psalm 63:1–8).

"I want to know Christ and the power of his resurrection and the sharing of his sufferings by becoming like him in his death" (Philippians 3:10).

"The God who made the world and everything in it, he who is Lord of heaven and earth, does not live in shrines made by human hands . . . since he himself gives to all mortals life and breath and all things. . . . So that they would search for God and perhaps grope for him and find him—though indeed he is not far from each one of us. For 'In him we live and move and have our being'" (Acts 17:24–25, 27–28).

Reflection Questions

CONSIDERATIONS FOR PRAYER

- When did I begin to be aware of my desire to find God?
- How have I nourished my desire for God?
- What happens when I remember that God desires me more than I desire God?
- How do feelings of loneliness or incompleteness turn me to God?
- What desires can blunt the vitality of my desire for God?

DISCERNMENT WITHIN A RELATIONSHIP

- How does my desire for God influence my choices within a relationship?
- Am I reverent with another's desire for God?
- Do I recognize the desire for God that underlies my human sexual desire?

Further Resources

Job 19:25–26

John 1:37–41

AA 7, 413

GS 57, 232

- Am I learning to attend to my desires for God as I make plans in my life?

DISCERNMENT WITHIN A GROUP ～

- Do we acknowledge that one of the purposes of our group is to help each other find, love, and serve God?

A DISCERNING RELATIONSHIP WITH THE WORLD ～

- How are world events affecting my awareness of the significance of the human desire for God?

Vatican Council II

"Human dignity rests above all on the fact that humanity is called to communion with God" (GS 19, 180).

"Nor is God remote from those who in shadows and images seek the unknown God, since he gives to everyone life and breath and all things and since the Savior wills everyone to be saved. Those who, through no fault of their own, do not know the Gospel of Christ or his church, but who nevertheless seek God with a sincere heart, and, moved by grace, try in their actions to do his will as they know it through the dictates of their conscience—these too may attain eternal salvation. Nor will divine providence deny the assistance necessary for salvation to those who, without any fault of theirs, have not yet arrived at an explicit knowledge of God, and who, not without grace, strive to lead a good life. Whatever of good or truth is found amongst them is considered by the church to be a preparation for the Gospel and given by him who enlightens all men and women that they may at length have life" (LG 16, 22).

Reverence

· · · · · · · · · · · ·

Reverence is the response given to any aspect of creation recognized as a gift of God. In reverence we bring awe and gratitude to all life and experience.

Ignatian Insights

"Human beings are created to praise, reverence and serve God Our Lord, and by means of doing this to save their souls. The other things on the face of the earth are created for human beings to help them in the pursuit of the end for which they are created. From this it follows that we ought to use these things to the extent that they help us toward our end, and free ourselves from them to the extent that they hinder us from it. To attain this it is necessary to make ourselves indifferent to all created things, in regard to everything which is left to our free will and is not forbidden" (*Spiritual Exercises*, 23).

". . . A mother and her daughter . . . joined him because they also were begging.

"Having reached a lodge, they came upon a great blaze with many soldiers at it, who gave them to eat, and a good deal of wine, coaxing them as if they wanted to warm them up. . . . At midnight, he heard loud cries there on top; getting up to see what it was, he found the mother and her daughter in the courtyard below, wailing and complaining that there was an attempt to violate them. At this such a strong feeling came over him that he began to shout, 'Must one put up with this?' and similar protests. He uttered these words with such force that all those in the house were startled and no one did him any harm" (*Autobiography*, 38–39).

Grace

To develop an attitude of reverence for the Word and action of God in whatever form it takes in my life.

Scripture

"O Lord, how manifold are your works! In wisdom you have made them all; the earth is full of your creatures. These all look to you to give them their food in due season; when you give to them, they gather it up; when you open your hand, they are filled with good things. When you send forth your spirit, they are created; and you renew the face of the ground. May the glory of the Lord endure forever; may the Lord rejoice in his works" (Psalm 104:24, 27–28, 30–31).

"Consider the lilies, how they grow: they neither toil nor spin; yet I tell you, even Solomon in all his glory was not clothed like one of these. But if God so clothes the grass of the field, which is alive today and tomorrow is thrown into the oven, how much more will he clothe you—you of little faith!" (Luke 12:27–28).

"Do you not know that you are God's temple and that God's Spirit dwells in you?" (1 Corinthians 3:16).

Reflection Questions

CONSIDERATIONS FOR PRAYER

- What experiences of beauty have called forth reverence from me?

- Have I prayed the Psalms as a way of growing in reverence for the ways of God?

- What motivates me to practice the self-discipline that reverence requires?

- Do I recognize and accept my sexuality reverently as a gift from God?

- In conversation with my spiritual director, have I explored any struggles with sexuality?

- What are the qualities or choices through which I show reverence toward myself and toward others?

Further Resources

1 Peter 3:15–16

2 Timothy 1:14

DISCERNMENT WITHIN A RELATIONSHIP ~

- When have I felt reverenced? Recall the circumstances and savor the effect that occasion had upon my sense of confidence in my identity.

- What happens interiorly when I try to be reverent with myself and another?

- How do I experience integration at this time of my life?

- How is reverence for sexuality helping me to integrate it into other aspects of my life?

- Do I celebrate the gift of sexuality with my spouse? Is there reverence in the expression of our sexuality?

- What behaviors in relationships do I find to be irreverent? Am I faithful about sharing that with another?

- Do I have the courage to seek the necessary support and counsel so I can counter any lack of reverence or even any subtle form of violence?

DISCERNMENT WITHIN A GROUP ~

- Is our reverence and respect for both men and women growing among us?

- What changes can we make to our way of being together in order to grow in reverence and respect?

- Are we learning to exercise power and appropriate control in ways that convey respect for others' thoughts, feelings, and diverse views?

A DISCERNING RELATIONSHIP WITH THE WORLD ~

- What local or national issues have as one of their causes a fundamental lack of reverence for human beings? For the earth?

Vatican Council II

"In virtue of its mission . . . (what is required of us is) first of all, to create in the church itself mutual esteem, reverence and harmony, and to acknowledge all legitimate diversity; in this way all who constitute the one people of God will be able to engage in ever more fruitful dialogue. . . . For the ties which unite the faithful together are stronger than those which separate them: Let there be unity in what is necessary, freedom in what is doubtful and charity in everything" (GS 92, 279–280).

Gentleness

•••••••••••••

The delicacy of the Spirit's action demands a gentleness that opens us to deeper attentiveness to God's call and invitation. Gentleness, which requires great inner strength, counters the movements toward arrogant power and aggressive assertiveness that can be prevalent in our environment.

Ignatian Insights

"If the giver of the Exercises sees that the one making them is experiencing desolation and temptation, he or she should not treat the retreatant severely or harshly, but gently and kindly. The director should encourage and strengthen the person for the future, unmask the deceptive tactics of the enemy of our human nature, and help the retreatant to prepare and dispose himself or herself for the consolation which will come" (*Spiritual Exercises*, 7).

"In this way, the Lord deigned that he awake as from sleep. As he now had some experience of the diversity of spirits from the lessons God had given him, he began to examine the means by which that spirit had come. He thus decided with great lucidity not to confess anything from the past any more; and so from that day forward he remained free of those scruples and held it for certain that Our Lord had mercifully deigned to deliver him" (*Autobiography*, 25).

Scripture

"Let your gentleness be known to everyone. The Lord is near" (Philippians 4:5).

"Who is wise and understanding among you? Show by your good life that your works are done with gentleness born of wisdom" (James 3:13).

Grace

To be gentle with myself and others as I grow in self-knowledge and learn to make better choices.

"I therefore, the prisoner in the Lord, beg you to lead a life worthy of the calling to which you have been called, with all humility and gentleness, with patience, bearing with one another in love, making every effort to maintain the unity of the Spirit in the bond of peace" (Ephesians 4:1–3).

"Now who will harm you if you are eager to do what is good? But even if you do suffer for doing what is right, you are blessed. Do not fear what they fear, and do not be intimidated, but in your hearts sanctify Christ as Lord. Always be ready to make your defense to anyone who demands from you an account of the hope that is in you; yet do it with gentleness and reverence. Keep your conscience clear, so that, when you are maligned, those who abuse you for your good conduct in Christ may be put to shame. For it is better to suffer for doing good, if suffering should be God's will, than to suffer for doing evil. For Christ also suffered for sins once for all, the righteous for the unrighteous, in order to bring you to God. He was put to death in the flesh, but made alive in the spirit" (1 Peter 3:13–18).

Reflection Questions

CONSIDERATIONS FOR PRAYER

- When have I been conscious of the Spirit's gift of gentleness at work in my life?
- How do I handle the disappointment I may feel when I have not done something well?
- Have I accepted the stereotype that suggests gentleness is a sign of weakness?
- What strength is called forth from me when I try to be gentle with myself and others?

Further Resources

Matthew 19:13

Galatians 5:22–25; 6:1

2 Timothy 2:22–25

Spiritual Exercises 18

LG 67, 89

DISCERNMENT WITHIN A RELATIONSHIP ~

- What opportunities do I have to practice gentleness?
- How are we balancing the shared power in our relationship?

DISCERNMENT WITHIN A GROUP ~

- How do we work with deadlines and other times of stress?
- What is our strength as a group?
- Are we aware and open to the possibility that our group can be controlled by dynamics such as fear, human respect, anger, or arrogance? Do we ever use our unity to exclude others?

A DISCERNING RELATIONSHIP WITH THE WORLD ~

- Who are the frail and fragile human beings who especially evoke gentleness from me?
- In a culture that holds speed as a value, how do I make time to hold my life gently rather than harshly?
- How do I practice gentleness toward the earth and use my power to foster shared responsibility for it?

Vatican Council II

"The liberty and dignity of the person helped must be respected with the greatest sensitivity. Purity of intention should not be stained by any self-seeking or desire to dominate. The demands of justice must first of all be satisfied; what is already due in justice is not to be offered as a gift in charity" (AA 8, 415).

Prayer

Prayer opens us to the mystery who is God, and serves essentially to turn our focus from self and our own plans to God's words, actions, and desires in our life and in the life of the world. In prayer, we praise God and express our gratitude, sorrow, and need.

Ignatian Insights

"On the road [to Onate] he persuaded him [his brother] to join in a vigil at Our Lady of Aranzazu. That night he prayed there that he might gain fresh strength for his journey" (*Autobiography*, 13).

"The method which he followed while he was drafting the Constitutions was to say Mass each day and to present to God the point that he was treating, and to pray over it; he always had tears at prayer and at Mass" (*Autobiography*, 101).

Prayer: "The Preparatory Prayer is to ask God Our Lord for grace that all my intentions, actions and operations may be directed purely to the service and praise of His Divine Majesty" (*Spiritual Exercises*, 46).

"A colloquy is made, properly speaking, in the way one friend speaks to another, or a servant to one in authority—now begging a favor, now accusing oneself of some misdeed, now telling one's concerns and asking counsel about them" (*Spiritual Exercises*, 54).

"For what fills and satisfies the soul consists, not in knowing much, but in our understanding the realities profoundly and in savoring them interiorly" (*Spiritual Exercises*, 2).

Grace

To make prayer a steady part of my decision making by bringing a prayerful attitude of heart to my daily decisions.

Scripture

"Therefore I prayed, and understanding was given me; I called on God, and the spirit of wisdom came to me" (Wisdom 7:7).

"Likewise the Spirit helps us in our weakness; for we do not know how to pray as we ought, but that very Spirit intercedes with sighs too deep for words. And God, who searches the heart, knows what is the mind of the Spirit, because the Spirit intercedes for the saints according to the will of God" (Romans 8:26–27).

"Whatever you ask for in prayer with faith, you will receive" (Matthew 21:22).

"Rejoice in hope, be patient in suffering, persevere in prayer" (Romans 12:12).

Reflection Questions

CONSIDERATIONS FOR PRAYER

- What has characterized my prayer journey over the course of my life?

- What memories do I have of God responding to my prayer?

- What strengthens my commitment to prayer now? What daily or weekly rhythm have I chosen for prayer?

- What helps me to quiet down enough to be still, listening, aware, and attentive in a prayerful presence to God?

- What does it mean for me to pray about something?

- What graces do I need to pray for in order to become more discerning in my life?

Further Resources

Matthew 6:6–15

John 15:7

1 Thessalonians 5:17

Sacrosanctum Concilium 12

Spiritual Exercises 12

DISCERNMENT WITHIN A RELATIONSHIP ～

- What dimension of our relationship is drawing me to prayer at this time?

- What am I noticing in that prayer? How do I interpret it?

DISCERNMENT WITHIN A GROUP ～

- Do we include prayer in our personal preparation for our gatherings?

- Have we found ways of praying together that are inclusive of the various ways in which we each prefer to pray?

- Are we praying for God's action among us as a group? Do we bring our real concerns for the group's growth to prayer?

A DISCERNING RELATIONSHIP WITH THE WORLD ～

- How do the cares of the world enter my prayer? Do I read the newspaper in a prayerful way?

- Have I learned how to pray about the troubling events in the world in ways that allow me to be both honest about my concerns and trusting of God's care for the world?

- Have I ever had an opportunity to pray with people of another religious tradition? What impact did that have on me and my way of praying?

Vatican Council II

"Human dignity rests above all on the fact that humanity is called to communion with God" (GS 19, 180).

". . . Christ is always present in his church, especially in liturgical celebrations. . . . He is present in his word since it is he himself who speaks when the holy scriptures are read. . . . Lastly, he is present when the church prays and sings, for he has promised 'where two or three are gathered together in my name there am I in the midst of them'" (SC 7, 120–121).

"Today, in many parts of the world, under the influence of the grace of the Holy Spirit, many efforts are being made in prayer, word and action to attain that fullness of unity which Jesus Christ desires" (Decree on Ecumenism, UR 4, 504).

"We cannot truly pray to God the Father of all if we treat any people as other than sisters and brothers, for all are created in God's image. People's relation to God the Father and their relation to other women and men are so dependent on each other that the Scripture says 'they who do not love, do not know God'" (NA 5, 574).

Gratitude

· · · · · · · · · · ·

Gratitude for the ways in which God has been active in our life encourages us to trust that God will continue to give the gifts we will need in the future. Gratitude for the blessings of God within and around us deepens as we grow in discernment.

Ignatian Insights

"This is an exclamation of wonder and surging emotion, uttered as I reflect on all creatures and wonder how they have allowed me to live and have preserved me in life. The angels: How it is that, although they are the sword of God's justice, they have borne with me, protected me, and prayed for me? The saints: How is it that they have interceded and prayed for me? Likewise, the heavens, the sun, the moon, the stars and the elements; the fruits, birds, fishes and animals. And the earth: How is it that it has not opened up and swallowed me. . . ?" (*Spiritual Exercises*, 60).

"*Colloquy*: I will also thank him because he has shown me, all through my life up to the present moment, so much pity and mercy" (*Spiritual Exercises*, 71).

"I will consider how all good things and gifts descend from above . . . as rays come down from the sun, or rains from their source" (*Spiritual Exercises*, 237).

Scripture

"On the way to Jerusalem Jesus was going through the region between Samaria and Galilee. As he entered a village, ten lepers approached him. Keeping their distance, they called out, saying, 'Jesus, Master, have mercy on us!' When he saw them, he said to them, 'Go and show yourselves to the priests.' And as they went, they were

Grace

To grow in gratitude for the ways that God is lovingly present to me at each moment of my life.

made clean. Then one of them, when he saw that he was healed, turned back, praising God with a loud voice. He prostrated himself at Jesus' feet and thanked him. And he was a Samaritan. Then Jesus asked, 'Were not ten made clean? But the other nine, where are they? Was none of them found to return and give praise to God except this foreigner?' Then he said to him, 'Get up and go on your way; your faith has made you well'" (Luke 17:11–19).

"Let the word of Christ dwell in you richly; teach and admonish one another in all wisdom; and with gratitude in your hearts sing psalms, hymns, and spiritual songs to God" (Colossians 3:16).

Reflection Questions

CONSIDERATIONS FOR PRAYER

- What do I discover as I recall God's gifts at the end of each day?
- What gifts of God stand out in my mind as especially formative of who I am?
- Am I grateful for the core faith experiences in my life?
- What aspects of my life do I find difficult to accept with gratitude? Am I aware of the way in which that lack of gratitude can hinder my openness to God's action in that aspect of my life?

DISCERNMENT WITHIN A RELATIONSHIP

- Do I pray in gratitude for those whom God has placed in my life?
- For what do I find myself consistently grateful in this relationship? What does that say to me?

Further Resources

Colossians 2:6–7

Colossians 3:12–17

DISCERNMENT WITHIN A GROUP ∽

- Do we find ourselves grateful for each other and our shared experience even at stressful times?

- Is our service characterized by a spirit of gratitude?

A DISCERNING RELATIONSHIP WITH THE WORLD ∽

- For what international developments am I especially grateful? Am I ready and willing to express my gratitude in action?

- Is my growing global consciousness increasing my gratitude for the wondrous action of God in diverse peoples and places?

Vatican Council II

"Allotting . . . gifts 'at will to each individual' . . . [the Spirit] also distributes special graces among the faithful of every rank. By these gifts, [the Spirit] makes them fit and ready to undertake various tasks and offices for the renewal and building up of the church, as it is written, 'the manifestation of the Spirit is given to everyone for profit.' Whether these charisms be very remarkable or more simple and widely diffused, they are to be received with thanksgiving and consolation since they are primarily suited to and useful for the needs of the church" (LG 12, 17).

"There is an imperative need for the individual apostolate in those areas where the church's freedom is seriously diminished. In such difficult circumstances the laity take over as far as possible the work of priests, jeopardizing their own freedom and sometimes their lives. . . . The council renders God most heartfelt thanks that in our own times he is still raising up lay people of heroic courage in the midst of persecution" (AA 17, 425).

Trust

· · · · · ·

Trust in God's everlasting desire to re-create the world in Christ is foundational to discerning the ways in which we can be an instrument of God's love in the world. Without trust in God, our efforts to be trusting and trustworthy will falter when we encounter human limitation or sinfulness in ourselves or others. Trust is the openness to creative possibilities.

Ignatian Insights

"All who spoke to him, on discovering that he did not carry any money for Jerusalem, began to dissuade him from making that trip, asserting with many arguments that it was impossible to find passage without money. But he had great assurance in his soul and he could not doubt but that he would in fact find a way to go to Jerusalem. . . . He did have six or seven ducats which had been given him for the passage from Venice to Jerusalem. . . . After leaving Rome, he began to realize that this was a lack of trust on his part, and it greatly bothered him that he had accepted them, so he . . . decided to give them generously to those who approached him, who were beggars usually" (*Autobiography*, 40).

"One who is in consolation should consider how he or she will act in future desolation, and store up new strength for that time" (*Spiritual Exercises*, Rules for Discernment, 323).

"God Our Lord knows our nature infinitely better than we do" (*Spiritual Exercises*, 89).

"When we are in desolation we should think that the Lord has left us to our own powers in order to test us, so that we may prove ourselves by resisting the various

Grace

To grow in my ability to trust the dynamic action of the Spirit of God within human beings, human affairs, and the marvels of creation.

87

agitations and temptations of the enemy. For we can do this with God's help, which always remains available, even if we do not clearly perceive it. Indeed, even though the Lord has withdrawn from us his abundant fervor, augmented love, and intensive grace, he still supplies sufficient grace for our eternal salvation" (*Spiritual Exercises*, Rules for Discernment, 320).

Scripture

"Commit your way to the Lord; trust in him, and he will act" (Psalm 37:5).

"When I am afraid, I put my trust in you" (Psalm 56:3).

"Trust in the Lord and keep at your job; for it is easy in the sight of the Lord to make the poor [person] rich suddenly, in an instant" (Sirach 11:21).

"Let me hear of your steadfast love in the morning, for in you I put my trust. Teach me the way I should go, for to you I lift up my soul" (Psalm 143:8).

"He said to his disciples . . . 'Do not worry about your life, what you will eat, or about your body, what you will wear. For life is more than food, and the body more than clothing. Consider the ravens: they neither sow nor reap, they have neither storehouse nor barn, and yet God feeds them. Of how much more value are you than the birds! And can any of you by worrying add a single hour to your span of life? If then you are not able to do so small a thing as that, why do you worry about the rest?'" (Luke 12:22–26).

Reflection Questions

CONSIDERATIONS FOR PRAYER

- What have been significant times in my life when I have had to trust God?
- What scriptural figures catch my attention because of their trust in God?

- What do I notice about my prayer when I am trusting God?
- How have I learned to trust others? What are signals to me that I am moving toward not trusting God or others?
- What types of experiences have shown me that God works in and through me?
- With what ease do I trust God at work in others as well as in myself?

DISCERNMENT WITHIN A RELATIONSHIP ~

- What has challenged us to be more trusting in our relationship?
- When I trust another, do I remember that he or she is also fragile and limited?
- Have I learned to forgive when my trust is betrayed?
- Am I growing in honesty and vulnerability by addressing any patterns of avoidance?
- How does our mutual trust help us to confront rather than avoid issues?

DISCERNMENT WITHIN A GROUP ~

- How do we balance trust in others with a healthy independence of thought and action? Are we learning to be interdependent within the group?
- Is our trust in each other strong and realistic enough that we can let go of controlling events and decisions when necessary?

A DISCERNING RELATIONSHIP WITH THE WORLD ~

- When I reflect on the massive migration of peoples globally, what do I discover about the significance of trusting and the responsibility of being trustworthy?
- Do I allow fear to overpower my desire to seek justice in particular situations?

Vatican Council II

" . . . Peace must be born of mutual trust between peoples instead of being forced on nations through dread of arms. . . . This task of supreme love for humanity which is the resolute building up of a lasting peace . . . demands that they enlarge their thoughts and their spirit beyond the confines of their own country, that they put aside nationalistic selfishness and ambitions to dominate other nations, and that they cultivate deep reverence for the whole of humanity. . . . Every one of us needs a change of heart" (GS 82, 269–270).

"Peace is more than the absence of war: it cannot be reduced to the maintenance of a balance of power between opposing forces nor does it arise out of despotic dominion, but it is appropriately called 'the effect of righteousness' (Is 32:17). It is the fruit of that right ordering of things . . . and . . . must be brought about by humanity in its thirst for an ever more perfect reign of justice. . . . Peace will never be achieved once and for all, but must be built up continually" (GS 78, 263).

THE DISCERNMENT PROCESS:
Interior Freedom

Interior freedom is a necessary condition and prior disposition for discernment.

A fruit of reflection and prayer is an awareness of one's interior freedom—that free access to one's being and life which opens to God who has first entrusted us with the gift of personal freedom. Our awareness of interior freedom may be faint at first because many expectations, demands, biases, and sinful patterns have served to hide that precious gift from our view. As we open ourselves more to God's action, our interior freedom will grow and develop through our daily choices to respond to God's grace as Jesus did. We will become more free to be ourselves, to live more by faith, to change and grow even when that involves loss.

Within discernment, we especially need to become free enough to be moved by the Spirit and to commit to the action which seems to be God's call to us. Ignatius saw the importance of making each decision with interior freedom. He offers guidance to us for those times when we realize that we have made an earlier decision without interior freedom.

In the case of an unchangeable election, once it has been made there is nothing further to elect, since the first one cannot be undone. Examples are marriage, priesthood, and the like. But if this election was not made properly and in a rightly ordered way, free from disordered affections, the only thing that can be considered is to repent and then explore how to lead a good life within the decision made. An election of this kind does not seem to be a divine vocation, since it is something improperly ordered and indirect. This is a way in which many are in error; for they take up a predisposed or bad choice and then regard it as a divine vocation. For every vocation from God is something pure, stainless, and without mingling of the flesh or any other poorly ordered affection (*Spiritual Exercises*, 172).

Recognition of one's unfreedom to choose God's way may emerge in painful ways—conflicts, frustrations, fears, resistances, moods, prejudices, and unforgiveness. Reflection and prayer about those apparently negative episodes in life can lead one to see in them God's unrelenting call to be free from all that would block one's becoming the person God calls one to be, regardless of circumstance or situation.

It is necessary [when making a good and sound election] to keep as my objective the end for which I am created, to praise God our Lord and save my soul. Furthermore, I ought to find myself indifferent, that is, without any disordered affection, to such an extent that I am not more inclined or emotionally disposed toward taking the matter proposed rather than relinquishing it, nor more toward relinquishing it rather than taking it. Instead, I should find myself in the middle, like the pointer of a balance, in order to be ready to follow that which I shall perceive to be more to the glory and praise of God our Lord and the salvation of my soul (*Spiritual Exercises*, 179).

God, who alone can free us, has promised freedom from all that would bind us. It is important to turn repeatedly to Jesus whose life, death, and resurrection carry God's gift and promise of the healing freedom we need and desire.

Reflection Questions

- When have you experienced the gift of interior freedom in your life?

- How does a consideration of your interior freedom—or lack of it—help you to name some of your experience in prayer and activity?

- Are you learning to notice patterns and connections within your ongoing experience?

- In what ways are you in need of more interior freedom so that you can be open and available to God's will in your life?

- What are some social and cultural issues where you personally experience darkness, blindness, or prejudice?

- What steps do you need to take to grow in the interior freedom needed to become a more discerning and just person?

MOMENT *of* CONFRONTATION

Annunciation

But she was much perplexed by his words and pondered what sort of greeting this might be.

~LUKE 1:29

Journey to Emmaus

"Moreover, some women of our group astounded us. They were at the tomb early this morning, and when they did not find his body there, they came back and told us that they had indeed seen a vision of angels who said that he was alive. Some of those who were with us went to the tomb and found it just as the women had said; but they did not see him. Then he said to them, 'Oh, how foolish you are, and how slow of heart to believe all that the prophets have declared!'"

~LUKE 24:22–25

Discernment draws us to the light, inviting us to live always in God's light and to move with God's light. So it is no surprise that our relationships with God and with others will include moments of confronting any potential places of darkness in the relationship. Discernment guides us through the acknowledgment of the darkness toward God's revealing light.

A growing knowledge of Christian faith, together with self-knowledge, will bring us to an awareness of the need for humility and courage as we gather and attend to the significant information that is essential for good decisions. The choices in this moment are crucially important for the future unfolding of our relationships and our growth in discernment.

Knowledge of Christian Faith

Discernment is predicated upon knowledge of the beliefs that shape the Christian community. Such knowledge is an invaluable guide to the interpretation of experience as we discern. It offers a critical grid for making the choices that help us to follow the way of Jesus.

Ignatian Insights

"With no worry at all, he persevered in his reading and his good resolutions; and all his time of conversation with members of the household he spent on the things of God; thus he benefited their souls. As he very much liked those books, the idea came to him to note down briefly some of the more essential things from the life of Christ and the saints; so he set himself very diligently to write a book . . . with red ink for the words of Christ, blue ink for those of Our Lady" (*Autobiography*, 11).

"For what fills and satisfies the soul consists, not in knowing much, but in our understanding the realities profoundly and in savoring them interiorly" (*Spiritual Exercises*, 2).

"Before entering into the deliberations about an election, a [person] who desires to become lovingly attached to the genuine teaching of Christ our Lord will profit much from considering and pondering the three ways of being humble . . ." (*Spiritual Exercises*, 164).

Grace

To deepen my appreciation of the tradition of Christian faith as a life-giving resource for my discernment and decision making.

Scripture

"Without any doubt, the mystery of our religion is great: He was revealed in flesh, vindicated in spirit, seen by angels, proclaimed among Gentiles, believed in throughout the world, taken up in glory" (1 Timothy 3:16).

"Mary treasured all these words and pondered them in her heart" (Luke 2:19).

"Then the king will say to those at his right hand, 'Come, you that are blessed by my Father, inherit the kingdom prepared for you from the foundation of the world; for I was hungry and you gave me food, I was thirsty and you gave me something to drink, I was a stranger and you welcomed me, I was naked and you gave me clothing, I was sick and you took care of me, I was in prison and you visited me.' Then the righteous will answer him, 'Lord, when was it that we saw you hungry and gave you food, or thirsty and gave you something to drink? And when was it that we saw you a stranger and welcomed you, or naked and gave you clothing? And when was it that we saw you sick or in prison and visited you?' And the king will answer them, 'Truly I tell you, just as you did it to one of the least of these who are members of my family, you did it to me'" (Matthew 25:34–40).

"For this is the message you have heard from the beginning, that we should love one another" (1 John 3:11).

Reflection Questions

CONSIDERATIONS FOR PRAYER

- What was my initial experience of being exposed to the Christian faith?
- When and under what circumstances did my formation in Christian faith take place?

Further Resources

Matthew 5:1–12

Colossians 2:6–8

Spiritual Exercises 170

Sacrosanctum Concilium, 5

Lumen Gentium, 62, 238–239

Christus Dominus 13, 290

- Who were the significant people in the process of my developing a mature understanding of the Christian faith? How have people passed on the faith to me?

- What were the circumstances surrounding my decision to take responsibility for developing this growing knowledge of the Christian faith?

- What academic experiences have contributed to my knowledge of the teachings of Christian faith?

- What efforts do I make to be a "lifelong learner" in the Christian faith?

- What practices such as reading scripture, attending lectures, or reading books on religious topics are part of my life now?

- Am I aware of the current teaching of the church through statements of church leaders?

- Have I learned how to bring prayerful and critical reflection to what I hear or read?

DISCERNMENT WITHIN A RELATIONSHIP ~

- Are we growing in our love of the Christian faith and its wisdom, even as it challenges our choices in our relationship?

DISCERNMENT WITHIN A GROUP ~

- Are we serious about improving our understanding of the aspects of Christian faith that are involved in our decisions?

- How is our Christian faith challenging us as a group?

A DISCERNING RELATIONSHIP WITH THE WORLD ~

- How are the needs of the earth and world reshaping my understanding of my Christian identity and responsibilities?

- What further ongoing education in my Christian faith do I need in order to be a more responsible citizen of the world?

Vatican Council II

"With the help of the Holy Spirit, it is the task of the whole people of God, particularly of its pastors and theologians, to listen to and distinguish the many voices of our times and to interpret them in the light of God's word, in order that the revealed truth may be more deeply penetrated, better understood, and more suitably presented" (GS 44, 215).

"The laity accomplish the church's mission in the world principally by that blending of behavior and faith which makes them the light of the world. . . . This apostolate should reach out to every . . . person in the environment and must not exclude any good, spiritual or temporal, that can be done for them. Genuine apostles are not content, however, with just that. They are also very serious about revealing Christ by word to those around them. It is a fact that many men and women cannot hear the Gospel and come to acknowledge Christ except through the lay people with whom they associate" (AA 13, 421–422).

"The search for truth, however, must be carried out in a manner that is appropriate to the dignity and social nature of the human person: that is, by free enquiry with the help of teaching or instruction, communication and dialogue. It is by these means that people share with each other the truth they have discovered, or think they have discovered, in such a way that they help one another in the search for truth. Moreover, it is by personal assent that they must adhere to the truth they have discovered" (Declaration on Religious Liberty, DH 3, 554).

Self-Knowledge

Discernment is concerned with moving more consistently into the light that God gives. This light will gently call us to honesty and humility before God. Self-knowledge keeps our discernment based in human reality. It is also essential to the recognition of our responses and resistances to God.

Ignatian Insights

"If the [person] feels an affection or inclination to something in a disordered way, it is profitable for that person to strive with all possible effort to come over to the opposite of that to which he or she is wrongly attached . . . that one's motive in desiring one thing rather than another will now be only the service, honor and glory of the Divine Majesty" (*Spiritual Exercises*, 16).

"In the case of persons who are earnestly purging away their sins, and who are progressing from good to better in the service of God our Lord . . . it is characteristic of the evil spirit to cause gnawing anxiety, to sadden, and to set up obstacles. In this way he unsettles these persons by false reasons aimed at preventing their progress.

"But with persons of this type it is characteristic of the good spirit to stir up courage and strength, consolations, tears, inspirations, and tranquility. He makes things easier and eliminates all obstacles, so that the persons may move forward in doing good" (*Spiritual Exercises*, Rules for Discernment, 315).

"To use still another comparison, the enemy acts like a military commander who is attempting to conquer and plunder his objective . . . . studies the strength and structure of a fortress, and then attacks at its weakest point. In the same way, the enemy of human nature . . . probes all our . . . virtues. Then at the point

Grace

To be open to God's ongoing gift of self-knowledge, especially to what I can learn about myself through prayerful reflection upon my past and present experiences, choices, and decisions.

where he finds us weakest and most in need . . . there he attacks. . ." (*Spiritual Exercises*, Rules for Discernment, 327).

"He did not notice this [difference], however; nor did he stop to ponder the distinction until the time when his eyes were opened a little, and he began to marvel at the difference and to reflect upon it, realizing from experience that some thoughts left him sad and others joyful. Little by little he came to recognize the difference between the spirits that were stirring . . ." (*Autobiography*, 8).

Scripture

"Therefore I prayed, and understanding was given me; I called on God, and the spirit of wisdom came to me" (Wisdom 7:7).

"O Lord, you have searched me and known me. . . . You discern my thoughts from far away. You search out my path . . . and are acquainted with all my ways. . . . Search me, O God, and know my heart; test me and know my thoughts" (Psalm 139:1–3, 23).

"These things God has revealed to us through the Spirit; for the Spirit searches everything, even the depths of God. For what human being knows what is truly human except the human spirit that is within? So also no one comprehends what is truly God's except the Spirit of God. Now we have received not the spirit of the world, but the Spirit that is from God, so that we may understand the gifts bestowed on us by God" (1 Corinthians 2:10–12).

Reflection Questions

CONSIDERATIONS FOR PRAYER

- What experiences in my childhood have especially shaped my views of God, of others, of myself?

Further Resources

Exodus 31:3

Luke 10:21

Mark 2:8

- What did I learn before the age of twenty-one that has become a strength to me? . . . that has hampered my adult growth?

- What have I learned through transitions?

- How dependent am I upon others' opinion for my self-confidence?

- How do I express myself and interact with others when I am receiving feedback that challenges my self-understanding?

- With what ease or difficulty do I accept my life transitions, limitations, mistakes, and sinfulness?

- Have I learned how to stay aware of my biases (both negative and positive) so that they do not prompt immediate nonreflective action?

- What interior movements and external behaviors make me aware that I am resisting or rejecting some self-knowledge? Am I learning to receive self-knowledge with humility?

- What do I tend to do when I am confused or surprised by an experience or the self-knowledge it gives me?

DISCERNMENT WITHIN A RELATIONSHIP ∾

- Do I find in this relationship someone who can mirror back to me some of my limits and gifts in ways that help me to grow?

- What happens for me when I reflect upon a shared ordinary daily experience? What difference does such reflection make in the way our relationship unfolds?

- Have we made time to reflect upon our relationship from the perspective of how God is transforming us in the midst of the relationship?

- How are we helping each other grow in self-knowledge?

DISCERNMENT WITHIN A GROUP ∾

- What are we learning about ourselves as a group as we try to become more discerning?

- What happens to our experience as a group when we share reflections about the prejudices that contribute to justice and injustice?

- Are we able to claim the challenging self-knowledge that may result?

- What do we discover about our need for interior freedom in the face of multiple views?

A DISCERNING RELATIONSHIP WITH THE WORLD ∾

- How do I maintain a sense of my authentic self when bombarded by stereotypes of people in roles such as mine?

- What feelings and desires are stirred in me when I reflect on world issues from the perspective of my Christian vocation? Am I open to being purified of my biases?

Vatican Council II

"Now for the first time in history people are not afraid to think that cultural benefits are for all and should be available to everybody. These claims are but the sign of a deeper and more widespread aspiration. Women and men as individuals and as members of society crave a life that is full, autonomous, and worthy of their nature as human beings; they long to harness for their own welfare the immense resources of the modern world. . . . In the light of the foregoing factors there appears the dichotomy of a world that is at once powerful and weak, capable of doing what is noble and what is base, disposed to freedom and slavery, progress and decline, amity and hatred. People are becoming conscious that the forces they have unleashed are in their own hands and that it is up to themselves to control them or be enslaved by them. Here lies the modern dilemma" (GS 9, 170–171).

Humility

Teresa of Avila's statement, "Humility is truth," points to a recognition that discernment is a human process, carried out in faith by people who seek God and recognize clearly that they are not God. Humility is a stance of truth we take in relationship to God, others, self, and the universe. Humility helps us make a decision in the midst of the partial, the provisional, and the imperfect that characterize our life.

Ignatian Insights

"A step or two away from the place where I will make my contemplation or meditation, I will stand for the length of an Our Father. I will raise my mind and think how God Our Lord is looking at me, and other such thoughts. Then I will make an act of reverence or humility" (*Spiritual Exercises*, 75).

"One who is in consolation ought to humble . . . herself or himself as much as possible, and reflect how little she or he is worth in time of desolation when that grace or consolation is absent" (*Spiritual Exercises*, Rules for Discernment, 324).

"With or by means of a preceding cause, both the good angel and the evil angel are able to cause consolation in the soul, but for their contrary purposes. The good angel acts for the progress of the soul, that it may grow and rise from what is good to what is better. The evil angel works for the contrary purpose, that is, to entice the soul to his own damnable intention and malice" (*Spiritual Exercises*, Rules for Discernment, 331).

Grace

To embrace my finitude and limits with gentleness and trust while confiding in God's generous goodness to me.

Scripture

"He called a child, whom he put among them, and said, 'Truly I tell you, unless you change and become like children, you will never enter the kingdom of heaven. Whoever becomes humble like this child is the greatest in the kingdom of heaven. Whoever welcomes one such child in my name welcomes me'" (Matthew 18:2–5).

" . . . Be of the same mind, having the same love, being in full accord and of one mind. Do nothing from selfish ambition or conceit, but in humility regard others as better than yourselves. Let each of you look not to your own interests, but to the interests of others. Let the same mind be in you that was in Christ Jesus, who, though he was in the form of God, did not regard equality with God as something to be exploited, but emptied himself, taking the form of a slave, being born in human likeness. And being found in human form, he humbled himself and became obedient to the point of death—even death on a cross. Therefore God also highly exalted him and gave him the name that is above every name, so that at the name of Jesus every knee should bend. . . ." (Philippians 2:2–11).

"Finally, all of you, have unity of spirit, sympathy, love for one another, a tender heart, and a humble mind" (1 Peter 3:8).

"All of you must clothe yourselves with humility in your dealings with one another, for 'God opposes the proud, but gives grace to the humble'" (1 Peter 5:5).

Reflection Questions

CONSIDERATIONS FOR PRAYER

- Does my understanding of humility include my relationship with God?

Further Resources

Luke 18:9–14

Ephesians 4:1–3

- What false understandings of humility have I rejected as blocking a wholesome self-understanding?

- When I remember God's generous fidelity toward me, what happens to my humility?

- What personal limits keep me healthily off-balance and especially relying upon God?

- If I have any addictions, have I admitted them with honesty and humility?

- How am I integrating humility and truthfulness into my practice of ministry or in my career?

- Have I noticed that making acts of humility can, over a period of time, develop a life-stance of humility within me?

DISCERNMENT WITHIN A RELATIONSHIP ∾

- What is the difference between listening for information and listening for the sake of reverencing God's action in the person and the conversation?

- What have been the challenges of integrating humility into our relationship?

DISCERNMENT WITHIN A GROUP ∾

- Regardless of the benefits or prestige that accrue to us as a group, what is our commitment to incorporating humility in our stance toward each other and to other individuals and groups?

- What helps us to guard against taking a stance toward others that is defensive or arrogant?

- What have the complexities of life in a global community revealed to me about the need for humility?

- How has my own commitment to humility developed as world events have unfolded during my lifetime?

Vatican Council II

"There can be no ecumenism worthy of the name without interior conversion. For it is from the newness of attitudes of mind, from self-denial and unstinted love, that desires of unity take their rise and develop in a mature way. We should therefore pray to the Holy Spirit for the grace to be genuinely self-denying, humble, gentle in the service of others and to have an attitude of generosity toward them. The Apostle of the Gentiles says: 'I, therefore, a prisoner for the Lord, beg you to lead a life worthy of the calling to which you have been called, with all humility and meekness, with patience, forbearing one another in love, eager to maintain the unity of the spirit in the bond of peace' (Eph. 4:1–3)" (OR 7, 508).

Courage

Courage is a virtue that can counter the fear experienced in life. God's invitations carry with them the promise of fidelity and help as we respond with openness and generosity to God's call.

Ignatian Insights

"God gave him great confidence that he would endure easily all the insults and injuries they might inflict" (*Autobiography*, 71).

"He (Ignatius) wanted to sail to Genoa but good friends . . . begged him not to. . . . Although they did say many things, enough to frighten him, nevertheless nothing made him hesitate. Boarding a large ship, he passed through a storm . . . (and) he was on the point of death three times" (*Autobiography*, 90).

"Although we ought not to change our former resolutions in time of desolation, it is very profitable to make vigorous changes in ourselves against the desolation, for example, by insisting more on prayer, meditation, earnest self-examination, and some suitable way of doing penance" (*Spiritual Exercises*, Rules for Discernment, 319).

"One who is in desolation should reflect that with the sufficient grace already available he or she can do much to resist all hostile forces, by drawing strength from our Creator and Lord" (*Spiritual Exercises*, Rules for Discernment, 324).

"The enemy . . . is weak when faced by firmness but strong in the face of acquiescence. . . . The enemy characteristically . . . loses courage, and flees with his

Grace

To be courageous in facing the challenges or difficulties that may be part of responding to what I discern to be God's call in my life.

temptations when the person engaged in spiritual endeavors stands bold and unyielding against the enemy's temptations and goes diametrically against them." (*Spiritual Exercises*, Rules for Discernment, 325).

Scripture

"'You are my servant, I have chosen you and not cast you off'; do not fear, for I am with you, do not be afraid, for I am your God; I will strengthen you, I will help you . . .' says the LORD; 'your Redeemer is the Holy One of Israel'" (Isaiah 41:9–10, 14).

"I believe that I shall see the goodness of the LORD in the land of the living. Wait for the LORD; be strong, and let your heart take courage; wait for the LORD!" (Psalm 27:13–14).

"When the days drew near for him to be taken up, he set his face to go to Jerusalem" (Luke 9:51).

"A windstorm arose on the sea, so great that the boat was being swamped by the waves; but he was asleep. And they went and woke him up, saying, 'Lord, save us! We are perishing!' And he said to them, 'Why are you afraid, you of little faith?' Then he got up and rebuked the winds and the sea; and there was a dead calm. They were amazed, saying, 'What sort of man is this, that even the winds and the sea obey him?'" (Matthew 8:24–27).

"Since, then, we have such a hope, we act with great boldness . . ." (2 Corinthians 3:12).

"For it is God who is at work in you, enabling you both to will and to work for his good pleasure" (Philippians 2:13).

Further Resources

Exodus 14:13–17, 21, 31

2 Maccabees 1:3

Acts 4:31

Reflection Questions

CONSIDERATIONS FOR PRAYER

- What part have fear and doubt played in my life? What helps me to approach life with courage rather than with fear and doubt?

- What memories do I have of acting with courage? What helps me to balance courage and humility?

- What happens when I take my fears and doubts to God in prayer?

- What have I learned to do so that fear can neither block nor motivate my action?

DISCERNMENT WITHIN A RELATIONSHIP

- What dimensions of our relationships continually call forth courage from us?

- Am I aware of any destructive patterns in my relationships?

- What signs indicate to me that I need to curtail or terminate a relationship?

DISCERNMENT WITHIN A GROUP

- What aspect of our shared experience requires that we respond with courage?

- Am I aware of addictive or manipulative behavior in our group?

- Are there communication problems within our group? What can I do to counter possible resulting paralysis within the group?

- What steps are important to take to address these realities?

A DISCERNING RELATIONSHIP WITH THE WORLD

- What is the source of my courage for acting for justice in ways that may disturb others?

"In every age, the church carries the responsibility of reading the signs of the times and of interpreting them in the light of the Gospel, if it is to carry out its task. In language intelligible to every generation, it should be able to answer the ever-recurring questions which people ask about the meaning of this present life and of the life to come, and how one is related to the other. We must be aware of and understand the aspirations, the yearnings, and the often dramatic features of the world in which we live" (GS 4, 165).

"No less fervent a zeal on the part of lay people is called for today. . . . For continuing population increases, progress in science and technology, and growing interdependence between people worldwide have immensely enlarged the field of the lay apostolate, a field that is in great part open to the laity alone. These developments have in addition given rise to new problems which require the laity's careful attention. . . . The church can only with difficulty make its presence and action felt without the help of the laity. A sign of this urgent and many-faceted need is the manifest action of the Holy Spirit making lay people nowadays increasingly aware of their responsibility and encouraging them everywhere to serve Christ and the church" (AA 1, 403–404).

"As the laity by divine condescension have as their brother Christ . . . they also have as brothers those who have been placed in the sacred ministry. . . . As St. Augustine puts it so very well: 'When I am frightened by what I am to you, then I am consoled by what I am with you. To you I am the bishop, with you I am a Christian. The first is an office, the second a grace; the first a danger, the second salvation" (LG 32, 50–51).

THE DISCERNMENT PROCESS:
Struggle

Struggle is a normal though costly experience for developing a discerning heart.

In the title he gave to the Rules for Discernment of Spirits, Ignatius gives a brief but clear description of what one is actually discerning.

> . . . rules to aid us toward perceiving and understanding, at least to some extent, the various motions which are caused in the soul: the good motions that they may be received, and the bad that they may be rejected (*Spiritual Exercises*, Rules for Discernment, 313).

Implicit in that description is the fact that the movements of the different spirits within us will not always be tending in the same God-ward direction. At times we experience movements—even strong movements—which seem to carry us or urge us in ways which give precedence to ourselves, not to God. They seem to urge us to choose in ways that express our self-will, not God's gracious will.

Honest reflection on our lives will also bring to light times when we were moved toward and chose to move toward sinful ways. The effect of choosing anything in preference to God is desolation. The desolation may be mild or it may be intense, but it will be characterized by agitation and darkness of various types.

> About spiritual desolation: By [this kind of] desolation I mean everything which is the contrary of what was described in the Third Rule; for example, obtuseness of soul, turmoil within it, an impulsive motion toward low and earthly things, or disquiet from various agitations and temptations. These move one toward lack of faith and leave one without hope and without love. One is completely listless, tepid, and unhappy, and feels separated from our Creator and Lord. For just as consolation is contrary to desolation, so the thoughts which arise from consolation are likewise contrary to those which spring from desolation (*Spiritual Exercises*, Rules for Discernment, 317).

At other times, the movement of grace within us can be such that the choices for God's will before us seem to flow almost naturally and we choose with ease and serenity what we have discovered to be God's desire for us at a given time in our lives. Ignatius's description of the effect of such consolation is one with which we easily resonate.

It is characteristic of the good spirit to stir up courage and strength, consolations, tears, inspirations, and tranquility. He makes things easier and eliminates all obstacles, so that the persons may move forward in doing good (*Spiritual Exercises*, Rules for Discernment, 315).

He offers a suggestion for savoring the consolation with a view to future less consoling times. "One who is in consolation should consider how he or she will act in future desolation, and store up new strength for that time" (*Spiritual Exercises*, Rules for Discernment, 323).

Both consolation and desolation can be subtle and not immediately apparent to us in our own experience. For this reason it is helpful as we become more discerning, and especially at times of struggle, to talk with another person who is familiar with the ways of God.

St. Ignatius captured that wise choice when he wrote:

In a similar manner, when the enemy of human nature turns his wiles and persuasions upon an upright person, he intends and desires them to be received and kept in secrecy. But when the person reveals them to his or her good confessor or some other spiritual person who understands the enemy's deceits and malice, he is grievously disappointed. For he quickly sees that he cannot succeed in the malicious project he began, because his manifest deceptions have been detected (*Spiritual Exercises*, Rules for Discernment, 326).

We can be helped by a spiritual director who is able to reflect with us upon our experience of consolation and desolation. While another person cannot carry out my discernment, he or she can offer reflections which foster light on my experience and clarity about the true matter to be discerned.

With the wisdom borne of his own experience, Ignatius could write of the alternating rhythm of movements which we may experience.

The Second Time [for making a sound and good election] is present when sufficient clarity and knowledge are received from the experience of consolations and desolations, and from experience in the discernment of various spirits (*Spiritual Exercises*, 176).

In fact, Ignatius suggested that an experience of alternating movements when considering an option was a sort of "prime time" for discerning and making a decision. The movements may at first appear to swing from one side of the pendulum to the other—perhaps with some rapidity or some intensity. However, with prayer and reflection and some guidance from a wise, faith-filled person, one will begin to notice that the pendulum swings more steadily and more gently until, finally, one is at balance, at a sort of equilibrium in the face of an option. Then one is able to know from the certainty in one's spirit that one has found the response to the option which represents for oneself the will of God, the choice one must make.

> During these Spiritual Exercises, when a person is seeking God's will, it is more appropriate and far better that the Creator and Lord himself should communicate himself to the devout soul, embracing it in love and praise, and disposing it for the way which will enable the soul to serve him better in the future. Accordingly, the one giving the Exercises ought not to lean or incline in either direction but rather, while standing by like the pointer of a scale in equilibrium, to allow the Creator to deal immediately with the creature, and the creature with its Creator and Lord (*Spiritual Exercises*, 15).

Ignatius's use of the word "movement" can lead us to believe that the movements will always be smooth, steady, conscious, constructive, enlightened, and oriented toward God. An experience of discernment will show us that it is often quite the opposite. At times we may be bombarded by chaotic, or unconscious or destructive or erratic, movements within our hearts and spirit. Or we may find ourselves filled with self-centered dispositions of many types and other qualities that herald a deep lack of interior freedom. In honesty, we may have to say: I do not want what God wants—whatever that is. Such a statement reveals what

can be the depth of one's struggle to desire or choose or accept or surrender to God's will. It may happen several times within a discernment process and many times within a discerning life.

> When we are in desolation we should think that the Lord has left us to our own powers in order to test us, so that we may prove ourselves by resisting the various agitations and temptations of the enemy. For we can do this with God's help, which always remains available, even if we do not clearly perceive it. Indeed, even though the Lord has withdrawn from us his abundant fervor, augmented love, and intensive grace, he still supplies sufficient grace for our eternal salvation (*Spiritual Exercises*, Rules for Discernment, 320).

Always, the struggle holds a call to humility and to trust in God whose ways may appear mysterious to us. Like Solomon, we may be moved to ask God for the gift of a discerning heart.

> "Give your servant therefore an understanding mind to govern your people, able to discern between good and evil; for who can govern this your great people." It pleased the Lord that Solomon had asked this. God said to him, "Because you have asked this, and have not asked for yourself long life or riches, or for the life of your enemies, but have asked for yourself

understanding to discern what is right, I now do according to your word. Indeed I give you a wise and discerning mind; no one like you has been before you and no one like you shall arise after you" (1 Kings 3:9–12).

MOMENT *of* CONVERSION

Mary's Story

The angel said to her, "Do not be afraid, Mary, for you have found favor with God."

~LUKE 1:30

The Emmaus Story

"Was it not necessary that the Messiah should suffer these things and then enter into his glory?"

~LUKE 24:26

Central to God's plan for growth is the dynamic process of conversion through which our minds and hearts are gradually shaped to be the mind and heart of Jesus Christ. Truly Jesus Christ becomes normative for my life as I open to conversion. Self-discipline is required to make the often difficult choices in response to God's daily invitations. Through such faith-filled choices God transforms not only our minds and hearts, but also our relationships. The Moment of Conversion re-orients a relationship so that the persons can become progressively more interiorly free for service of the reign of God in the world.

Jesus Christ as Normative for My Life

Jesus Christ's entire life was a discernment to know and do the will of his Father. For Christians, Jesus' life, death, and resurrection is the normative pattern. Gradually, our discerned decisions draw us to a deeper likeness to Christ.

Ignatian Insights

"As he read them over many times [*The Life of Christ* and a book on the saints], he became rather fond of what he found written there. But interrupting his reading, he sometimes stopped to think about the things he had read and at other times about the things of the world that he used to think of before" (*Autobiography*, 6).

"His whole intention was to do such great external works because the saints had done so for the glory of God, without considering any more particular prospect" (*Autobiography*, 14).

"It is good to imagine Christ our Lord . . . to observe how he eats, how he drinks, how he looks about, and how he converses, and then to try to imitate him . . ." (*Spiritual Exercises*, 214).

"The third prelude will be to ask for what I desire: Here I will ask for the grace to choose that which is more to the glory of the Divine Majesty and the salvation of my soul" (*Spiritual Exercises*, 152).

"I wish and desire, and it is my deliberate decision, provided only that it is for your greater service and praise, to imitate you in bearing all injuries and affronts, and any poverty, actual as well as spiritual, if your Most Holy Majesty desires to choose and receive me into such a life and state" (*Spiritual Exercises*, 98).

Grace

To embrace the life-death-resurrection of Jesus as the pattern and norm for all aspects of my life.

Scripture

"After saying farewell to them, he went up on the mountain to pray" (Mark 6:46).

"Once when Jesus was praying alone, with only the disciples near him, he asked them, 'Who do the crowds say that I am?'" (Luke 9:18).

"Yet whatever gains I had, these I have come to regard as loss because of Christ. More than that, I regard everything as loss because of the surpassing value of knowing Christ Jesus my Lord. For his sake I have suffered the loss of all things, and I regard them as rubbish, in order that I may gain Christ and be found in him, not having a righteousness of my own that comes from the law, but one that comes through faith in Christ, the righteousness from God based on faith. I want to know Christ and the power of his resurrection and the sharing of his sufferings by becoming like him in his death, if somehow I may attain the resurrection from the dead. Not that I have already obtained this or have already reached the goal; but I press on to make it my own, because Christ Jesus has made me his own. . . . Let those of us then who are mature be of the same mind; and if you think differently about anything, this too God will reveal to you. Only let us hold fast to what we have attained" (Philippians 3:7–12, 15–16).

"Only, live your life in a manner worthy of the gospel of Christ . . . standing firm in one spirit, striving side by side with one mind for the faith of the gospel" (Philippians 1:27).

"And whatever you do, in word or deed, do everything in the name of the Lord Jesus, giving thanks to God the Father through him" (Colossians 3:17).

Further Resources

Luke 4:18–21

Romans 8:11

2 Corinthians 3:2–3

Reflection Questions

CONSIDERATIONS FOR PRAYER

- What answer would I give to Jesus' question, "Who do you say that I am?"
- How has my understanding of the person and mission of Jesus changed during my lifetime?
- Do I use Jesus as a reference point when making my decisions?
- Do I look at how closely my life follows the pattern of Jesus' life?
- What helps me to stay in tune with the liturgical seasons in which the life, death, and resurrection of Jesus unfold?
- To what qualities in the person of Jesus am I drawn at this time of my life?
- Do I want, with God's help, to develop those qualities in myself?
- What does the meaning of Jesus' suffering and death offer to my understanding of discernment?

DISCERNMENT WITHIN A RELATIONSHIP

- Which of Jesus' values are most difficult for me to practice in my relationships?
- Do I find peace, and maybe even joy, when I make a difficult choice that is in harmony with the values of Jesus?
- Do I make efforts to allow my relationships to reflect the significance of Jesus in my life?
- Has my commitment to Jesus Christ ever led me to end a relationship? How did that choice affect me and others?

DISCERNMENT WITHIN A GROUP ∿

- What values of Jesus are we especially being called to practice at this time?

- What is making it difficult for us to practice the values of Jesus? What supports us in doing that?

A DISCERNING RELATIONSHIP WITH THE WORLD ∿

- What other models of wholeness compete with Jesus Christ for a place as normative in my life?

Vatican Council II

"All are called to this union with Christ, who is the light of the world, from whom we come, through whom we live, and towards whom we direct our lives" (LG 3, 3).

"Human activity (work) is for the benefit of human beings. . . . People are of greater value for what they are than for what they have. Technical progress is of less value than advances towards greater justice, wider kinship and a more humane social environment. Technical progress may supply the material for human advance but it is powerless to achieve it" (GS 35, 200–201).

Metanoia

Becoming discerning will include the invitation to *metanoia*, a conversion of heart. As we make our way toward greater clarity about God's will, we will discover those places in our mind, heart, and life-patterns that must change so that our life will reflect the mind, heart, and actions of Jesus.

Ignatian Insights

"In the case of persons who are going from one mortal sin to another, the enemy ordinarily proposes to them apparent pleasures. He makes them imagine delights and pleasures of the senses, in order to hold them fast and plunge them deeper into their sins and vices. But with persons of this type the good spirit uses a contrary procedure. Through their good judgment on problems of morality he stings their consciences with remorse" (*Spiritual Exercises*, Rules for Discernment, 314).

"When the enemy of human nature has been perceived and recognized by . . . the evil end to which he is leading, it then becomes profitable for the person whom he has tempted in this way to examine the whole train of the good thoughts which the evil spirit brought to the soul; . . . how they began, and then how, little by little, the evil spirit endeavored to bring the soul down from the . . . spiritual joy in which it had been, and finally brought it to his own evil intention. The purpose is that through this experience, now recognized and noted, the soul may guard itself in the future against these characteristic snares" (*Spiritual Exercises*, Rules for Discernment, 334).

"Toward Amending and Reforming One's Own Life and State: It is very profitable [to have] a procedure and method . . . to improve and reform [one's life], by [considering] the purpose of each one's creation, life and state of life: the glory and praise of

Grace

To be open to the conversion of heart that I need in order to respond to God's daily, and sometimes surprising, calls to reflect the values of Jesus.

God our Lord and the salvation of their own soul. . . . In all this and by it, each one should desire and seek nothing except the greater praise and glory of God our Lord. For everyone ought to reflect that in all spiritual matters, the more one divests oneself of self-love, self-will, and self-interests, the more progress one will make" (*Spiritual Exercises*, 189).

"Yet there was this difference. When he was thinking of those things of the world, he took much delight in them, but afterwards, when he was tired and put them aside, he found himself dry and dissatisfied. But when he thought of going to Jerusalem barefoot, and of eating nothing but plain vegetables and of practicing all the other rigors that he saw in the saints, not only was he consoled when he had these thoughts but even after putting them aside he remained satisfied and joyful. He did not notice this, however; nor did he stop to ponder the distinction until the time when his eyes were opened a little, and he began to marvel at the difference and to reflect upon it, realizing from experience that some thoughts left him sad and others joyful. Little by little he came to recognize the difference between the spirits that were stirring, one from the devil, the other from God. "From this lesson he derived not a little light, and he began to think more earnestly about his past life and about the great need he had to do penance for it. . . . with as much of disciplines and fasts as a generous spirit, ablaze with God, would want to perform" (*Autobiography*, 8–9).

Scripture

"A new heart I will give you, and a new spirit I will put within you; and I will remove from your body the heart of stone and give you a heart of flesh" (Ezekiel 36:26).

"The word that came to Jeremiah from the LORD: 'Come, go down to the potter's house, and there I will let you hear my words.' So I went down to the potter's house, and there he was working at his wheel. The vessel he was making of clay was spoiled

Further Resources

Ezekiel 11:5,19–20

John 3:5

in the potter's hand, and he reworked it into another vessel, as seemed good to him. Then the word of the LORD came to me: Can I not do with you, O house of Israel, just as this potter has done? says the LORD. Just like the clay in the potter's hand, so are you in my hand, O house of Israel" (Jeremiah 18:1–6).

"I am the voice of one crying out in the wilderness, 'Make straight the way of the Lord'" (John 1:23).

"Peter said to them, 'Repent, and be baptized every one of you in the name of Jesus Christ so that your sins may be forgiven; and you will receive the gift of the Holy Spirit'" (Acts 2:38).

"For I do not do the good I want, but the evil I do not want is what I do . . . For I delight in the law of God in my inmost self, but I see in my members another law at war with the law of my mind, making me captive to the law of sin that dwells in my members. Wretched [person] that I am! Who will rescue me from this body of death? Thanks be to God through Jesus Christ our Lord!" (Romans 7:19, 22–25).

Reflection Questions

CONSIDERATIONS FOR PRAYER

- What have been God's ways of calling me to a conversion of heart at earlier times in my life?

- How have earlier experiences of conversion of heart helped me to become more truly my best self?

- What signs such as jealousy and lack of trust indicate to me that I may need a conversion of heart?

- Do I incorporate an expression of sorrow and a plea for mercy in my prayer when I become aware of my sinfulness?

- What is my resistance to God's call to surrender?

DISCERNMENT WITHIN A RELATIONSHIP ◌

- At this time in our relationship, what am I being asked to turn away from in order to turn more completely to the Lord?

- In what virtue am I called to grow at this time of my life in order to be more like the Lord?

DISCERNMENT WITHIN A GROUP ◌

- What attitudes or attachments are preventing us from being truly open to God's presence and action among us?

- What will be required of us as a group if we take ongoing conversion seriously?

A DISCERNING RELATIONSHIP WITH THE WORLD ◌

- What is my reaction to the suggestion that we need a conversion of heart and action in order to be respectful and just stewards of the goods of our planet?

- How are the poor and struggling people of the world calling me to a conversion of heart?

Vatican Council II

"Great numbers of people are acutely conscious of being deprived of the world's goods through injustice and unfair distribution and are vehemently demanding their share of them. . . . The hungry nations cry out to their affluent neighbors; women claim parity with men in fact as well as of right, where they have not already obtained it; laborers and agricultural workers insist not just on the necessities of life but also on the opportunity to develop by their labor their personal talents and to play their due role in organizing economic, social, political, and cultural life. Now for the first time in history people are not afraid to think that cultural benefits are for all and should be available to everybody" (GS 9, 170).

"Every renewal of the church essentially consists in an increase of fidelity to her own calling. Undoubtedly this explains the dynamism of the movement toward unity. Christ summons the church, as she goes her pilgrim way, to that continual reformation of which she always has need, insofar as she is a human institution here on earth. Consequently, if, in various times and circumstances, there have been deficiencies in moral conduct or in church discipline, or even in the way that church teaching has been formulated—to be carefully distinguished from the deposit of faith itself—these should be set right at the opportune moment and in the proper way" (UR 6, 507–508).

Self-Discipline

Self-discipline is a critical resource for discerning persons. With it, we can deny ourselves when God's call requires that loving sacrifice. It leads us to attend more carefully to our interior spiritual movements and motivation, to the steps in the discernment process and to the information related to our discernment.

Ignatian Insights

"If by chance the [person] feels an affection or inclination to something in a disordered way, it is profitable . . . to strive with all possible effort to come over to the opposite of that to which he or she is wrongly attached" (*Spiritual Exercises*, 16).

"It should be presupposed that every good Christian ought to be more eager to put a good interpretation on a neighbor's statement than to condemn it. Further, if one cannot interpret it favorably, one should ask how the other means it. If that meaning is wrong, one should correct the person with love; and if this is not enough, one should search out every appropriate means through which, by understanding the statement in a good way, it may be saved" (*Spiritual Exercises*, 22).

". . . There is merit if [one's] words are ordered to a good end . . ." (*Spiritual Exercises*, 40).

"Settle with oneself how much food is to be taken . . . and further, to do this every day. Then one should not exceed this amount either because of appetite or temptation . . ." (*Spiritual Exercises*, 217).

Grace

To develop a more disciplined approach in my daily life by means of my choices regarding things such as use of time, food and drink, consumer habits, and leisure patterns.

127

"There are three chief causes for the desolation in which we find ourselves. The first is that we ourselves are tepid, lazy, or negligent in our spiritual exercises. Thus the spiritual consolation leaves us because of our own faults" (*Spiritual Exercises*, Rules for Discernment, 322).

"When we abstain from what is superfluous we are practicing, not penance, but temperance. We practice penance when we abstain from what is ordinarily suitable" (*Spiritual Exercises*, 83).

Scripture

"Jesus, full of the Holy Spirit, returned from the Jordan and was led by the Spirit in the wilderness, where for forty days he was tempted by the devil. He ate nothing at all during those days, and when they were over, he was famished" (Luke 4:1–2).

"When Jesus heard this, he said to him, 'There is still one thing lacking. Sell all that you own and distribute the money to the poor, and you will have treasure in heaven; then come, follow me'" (Luke 18:22).

"And he said to them, 'Why are you sleeping? Get up and pray that you may not come into the time of trial'" (Luke 22:46).

Reflection Questions

CONSIDERATIONS FOR PRAYER

- How serious am I about giving more than lip service to my discipleship?
- Have I developed an attitude toward self-sacrifice that views it as a way of loving?
- In what areas of my life have I allowed a lack of self-discipline to take hold?
- What motivates me to practice the self-discipline which listening requires?
- Do I draw on habits of self-discipline when I find prayer is dry or boring?
- Have I thought of asking God to help me to grow as a self-disciplined person?

Further Resources

Luke 6:27–38

Spiritual Exercises 12

Gauduim et spes 10, 171

DISCERNMENT WITHIN A RELATIONSHIP ∽

- What am I learning about the role of self-discipline at those times when there is struggle or suffering in our relationship?

DISCERNMENT WITHIN A GROUP ∽

- Do we have sufficient self-discipline to deal patiently with the many facets within any controversy?

- Are we able to practice self-discipline without becoming rigid and unfeeling?

A DISCERNING RELATIONSHIP WITH THE WORLD ∽

- Is my self-discipline developed enough to allow me to bring understanding and compassion to those who differ from me?

- Would greater self-discipline free some of my time for local actions for justice?

Vatican Council II

"Therefore, the true minister of Christ is conscious of his own weakness and labors in humility. He tries to find out what is well-pleasing to God and, bound as it were in the Spirit, he is guided in all things by the will of him who wishes all women and men to be saved. He is able to discover and carry out that will in the course of his daily routine by humbly placing himself at the service of all those who are entrusted to his care by God, in the office that has been committed to him and the variety of events that make up his life. . . . By this humility and by responsible and willing obedience, priests conform themselves to Christ . . . who 'emptied himself, taking the form of a servant . . . and became obedient unto death' (Philippians 2:7–9)" (Decree on the Life and Ministry of Priests, PO 15, 349–350).

Response

While discernment is an ongoing process, it also requires, at times, a clear, specific, and decisive response to what we have discovered to be God's desire. Our response then initiates a time of implementation that itself calls for ongoing discernment.

Ignatian Insights

"We should pay close attention to the whole train of our thoughts. If the beginning, middle, and end are all good and tend toward what is wholly good, it is a sign of the good angel. But if the train of the thoughts which a spirit causes ends up in something evil or diverting, or in something less good than what the soul was originally proposing to do; or further, if it weakens, disquiets, or disturbs the soul, by robbing it of the peace, tranquility, and quiet which it enjoyed earlier, all this is a clear sign that this is coming from the evil spirit, the enemy of our progress and eternal salvation" (*Spiritual Exercises*, Rules for Discernment, 333).

"He also had many visions when he said Mass; and when he was drawing up the Constitutions too, he had them very often. He can now affirm this more easily because every day he wrote down what went on in his soul and he had it now in writing. He showed me a rather large bundle of writings, of which he read me a good bit. Most were visions that he saw in confirmation of some of the Constitutions, at times seeing God the Father, at times all three Persons of the Trinity, at times Our Lady—who interceded and at times confirmed" (*Autobiography*, 100).

"The method which he followed while he was drafting the Constitutions was to say Mass each day and to present to God the point that he was treating, and to pray over it; he always had tears at prayer and at Mass" (*Autobiography*, 101).

Grace

To become sensitive to the moment when discernment requires a response that seems to be the best possible action at this time.

"One who is in consolation should consider how he or she will act in future desolation, and store up new strength for that time" (*Spiritual Exercises*, Rules for Discernment, 323).

"The Fourth Rule. It is characteristic of the evil angel, who takes on the appearance of an angel of light, to enter by going along the same way as the devout soul and then to exit by his own way with success for himself. That is, he brings good and holy thoughts attractive to such an upright soul and then strives little by little to get his own way, by enticing the soul over to his own hidden deceits and evil intentions" (*Spiritual Exercises*, Rules for Discernment, 332).

"There are three chief causes for the desolation in which we find ourselves. . . . The second is that the desolation is meant to test how much we are worth and how far we will extend ourselves in the service and praise of God, even without much repayment by way of consolations and increased graces" (*Spiritual Exercises*, Rules for Discernment, 322).

Scripture

"Then Mary said, 'Here am I, the servant of the Lord; let it be with me according to your word'" (Luke 1:38).

"She said to him, 'Yes, Lord, I believe that you are the Messiah, the Son of God, the one coming into the world'" (John 11:27).

"Father, if you are willing, remove this cup from me; yet, not my will but yours be done" (Luke 22:42).

"'It is finished.' Then he bowed his head and gave up his spirit" (John 19:30).

"When they had finished breakfast, Jesus said to Simon Peter, 'Simon son of John, do you love me more than these?' He said to him, 'Yes, Lord; you know that I love you.' Jesus said to him, 'Feed my lambs'"(John 21:15).

Further Resources

Matthew 9:28

2 Corinthians 1:20

Spiritual Exercises 6

Reflection Questions

CONSIDERATIONS FOR PRAYER ~

- What helps me to remember that, while my response will be to some extent limited or imperfect, it can be used by God to carry out God's plan in my life?

- What feelings do I experience when I move toward an actual decision?

- Am I free enough to make my decision regardless of what other people may think of it?

- Have I continued to ask God to give me the interior freedom that I need to discover and carry out God's will?

- Do my daily responses keep me faithful to both my identity and the responsibilities of all of my relationships?

DISCERNMENT WITHIN A RELATIONSHIP ~

- Am I aware that I may have to respond in a way that will displease or disappoint someone who is important to me?

- Am I willing to trust that God will guide us through that painful moment?

DISCERNMENT WITHIN A GROUP ~

- How have we embraced the decisions we have made?

- Have we begun the hard work of implementing them?

A DISCERNING RELATIONSHIP WITH THE WORLD ~

- What responses am I making locally to contribute to just decisions for future generations?

"In each nation and social group there is a growing number of men and women who are conscious that they themselves are the architects and molders of their community's culture. All over the world the sense of autonomy and responsibility increases with effects of the greatest importance for the spiritual and moral maturity of humankind. This will become clearer to us if we advert to the unification of the world and the duty imposed on us to build up a better world in truth and justice. We are witnessing the birth of a new humanism, where people are defined before all else by their responsibility to their sisters and brothers and at the court of history" (GS 55, 230–231).

"The more the power of men and women increases the greater is their responsibility as individuals and as members of the community" (GS 34, 200).

THE DISCERNMENT PROCESS: Choices

Small decisions made during the discernment process affect the outcome of the discernment.

Choices are our response to God, to others, to oneself. They shape our life and often have significant consequences for the lives of others. The discernment process progresses choice by choice. Gradually, as we learn with the help of reflection, prayer, and Examen where and how God is inviting us to respond, our choices take on a more defining character and are marked by a more faith-filled quality.

In what may surprise us, Ignatius offers insight into an experience of desolation which may be present around the time when we are making a choice. These insights challenge "knee-jerk reactions" as well as our human urgency to find relief by resolving a matter.

During a time of desolation one should never make a change. Instead, one should remain firm and constant in the resolutions and in the decision which one had on the day before the desolation, or in a decision in which one was during a previous time of consolation. For just as the good spirit is chiefly the one who guides and counsels us in time of consolation, so it is the evil spirit who does this in time of desolation. By following his counsels we can never find the way to a right decision (*Spiritual Exercises,* Rules for Discernment, 318).

Although we ought not to change our former resolutions in time of desolation, it is very profitable to make vigorous changes in ourselves against the desolation, for example, by insisting more on prayer, meditation, earnest self-examination, and some suitable way of doing penance (*Spiritual Exercises*, Rules for Discernment, 319).

One who is in desolation should strive to preserve himself or herself in patience. This is the counterattack against the vexations which are being experienced. One should remember that after a while the consolation will return again, through the diligent efforts against the desolation . . . (*Spiritual Exercises*, Rules for Discernment, 321).

Our efforts to respond to a heightened awareness of our daily gifts and graces, as well as the needs of others, often lead us to a moment of choice. Our response to even an apparently simple invitation from God can open whole new areas of our life as a discerning person. Even though we may be aware of our lack of interior freedom, we are faced with a choice. While discerning a decision, attention to consolation and desolation is essential. This attentive fidelity will enable us to make a choice that allows us to respond to the gentle lead of God. This stands in marked contrast to a nonreflective reaction rooted in our expectations, frustrations, fears, or doubts. This discernment will require time and patience.

Reflection Questions

CONSIDERATIONS FOR PRAYER

- What new choices seem to be before me as I grow and become a more discerning person?

- What am I learning from reflection upon the choices that I make each day?

- Are the choices leading me to reframe the matters about which I am discerning?

- Can I recall a time when I had to wait for consolation before making a decision? What have I learned from that experience?

- Am I growing in faith in God's provident care as I deal with the limitations which are placed upon my choices?

- Do I ask for and give complete and accurate information so that choices in my personal and professional life can be informed decisions?

Moment *of* Reconciliation

Mary's Story

"And now, you will conceive in your womb and bear a son, and you will name him Jesus. He will be great, and will be called the Son of the Most High, and the Lord God will give to him the throne of his ancestor David. He will reign over the house of Jacob forever, and of his kingdom there will be no end."

~LUKE 1:31–33

The Emmaus Story

Then beginning with Moses and all the prophets, he interpreted to them the things about himself in all the scriptures.

~LUKE 24:27

In this Moment of Reconciliation, God gathers the fragments of our broken hopes and hearts, heals the wounds resulting from our limit-bound and, at times, sinful choices, and pulls us to our feet again. The strength to love is new—we've learned that love is possible again with God's help.

Discernment in this moment focuses our attention on God's ways of loving so that our loving will be characterized more and more by the compassion, patience, surrender, forgiveness, and healing we have experienced in Jesus. On our own faith journey, it is the life, death, and resurrection of Jesus that gives strength and meaning to our lives.

Patience

. . . .

Discernment, a process that unfolds over time, requires patient effort and unselfish care. God is not to be hurried, so we must lovingly embrace the process of moving with the light and the opportunities as God gives them.

Ignatian Insights

"He persevered in his reading and his good resolutions. . . . He often thought about his intention [to go to Jerusalem as a pilgrim] and wished he were now wholly well so he could get on his way" (*Autobiography*, 11).

"He told me that he had not composed the Exercises all at once, but that when he noticed some things in his soul and found them useful, he thought they might also be useful to others, and so he put them in writing: for example, the examination of conscience. . . . He told me that he derived the elections in particular from that diversity of spirit and thoughts which he had at Loyola when he was still suffering in the leg" (*Autobiography*, 99).

"(For as it happens) . . . some persons happen to be slower in finding what they are seeking, that is, contrition, sorrow, and tears for their sins. Similarly, some persons work more diligently than others, and are more pushed back and forth and tested by different spirits" (*Spiritual Exercises*, 4).

"One who is in desolation should strive to preserve himself or herself in patience. This is the counterattack against the vexations which are being experienced. One should remember that after a while the consolation will return again, through the diligent efforts against the desolation" (*Spiritual Exercises*, Rules for Discernment, 321).

Grace

To exercise the patience that is needed in order to attend to the unfolding action of God in myself, others, and the world around me.

Scripture

"[Mary] was much perplexed by his words and pondered what sort of greeting this might be" (Luke 1:29).

"We know that the whole creation has been groaning in labor pains until now; and not only the creation, but we ourselves, who have the first fruits of the Spirit, groan inwardly while we wait. . . . For in hope we were saved. Now hope that is seen is not hope. For who hopes for what is seen? But if we hope for what we do not see, we wait for it with patience" (Romans 8:22–25).

"But this I call to mind, and therefore I have hope: The steadfast love of the LORD never ceases, his mercies never come to an end; they are new every morning; great is your faithfulness. 'The LORD is my portion,' says my soul, 'therefore I will hope in him.' The LORD is good to those who wait for him, to the soul that seeks him. It is good that one should wait quietly for the salvation of the LORD" (Lamentations 3:21–26).

"Be patient, therefore, beloved, until the coming of the Lord. The farmer waits for the precious crop from the earth, being patient with it until it receives the early and late rains. You also must be patient" (James 5:7–8).

"May you be made strong with all the strength that comes from his glorious power, and may you be prepared to endure everything with patience" (Colossians 1:11).

"But for that very reason I received mercy, so that in me, as the foremost, Jesus Christ might display the utmost patience, making me an example to those who would come to believe in him for eternal life" (1 Timothy 1:16).

Further Resources

Romans 12:12

Romans 8:18–25

Reflection Questions

CONSIDERATIONS FOR PRAYER

- What steps can I take to slow my pace so that I can attend more fully to the action of God?

- What aspect of the life of Jesus helps me to be patient when results are not immediate?

- What lack of interior freedom can spark my impatience?

- What have I learned in my efforts to be more patient with limitation?

- What helps me to examine an experience of consolation or desolation rather than only to glance at it and move on?

- When have I experienced new self-awareness or insight coming to me slowly in a way that is almost imperceptible?

DISCERNMENT WITHIN A RELATIONSHIP

- What makes me aware of my need to attend more carefully to information shared, questions asked, or feelings expressed?

- How much patience do I have when waiting for others to give me the data I need for a decision?

- Can I recognize the difference between waiting patiently and resistance to taking action?

- How do I respond to anger in myself and in others?

DISCERNMENT WITHIN A GROUP ∼

- What degree of patience and thoroughness do we bring to reviewing any data that is part of our shared project or purpose?

- Are we patient with each other's questioning?

- While patience can be an appropriate response, what are other effective responses to stress or differences such as gender, race, viewpoints?

A DISCERNING RELATIONSHIP WITH THE WORLD ∼

- How have the developments in technology made patience more difficult for me?

- What steps can I take so that I do not make demands of persons, including God, in the same manner as I make demands of machines?

Vatican Council II

"They show themselves to be the children of the promise if, strong in faith and hope, they make the most of the present time (Eph 5:16; Col 4:5), and with patience await the future glory (see Rom 8:25). Let them not hide this hope then in the depths of their hearts, but rather express it through the structure of their secular lives in continual conversion . . ." (LG 35, 52–53).

"But by the power of the risen Lord it (the Church) is given strength to overcome, in patience and in love, its sorrows and its difficulties, both those that are from within and those that are from without, so that it may reveal in the world, faithfully, although with shadows, the mystery of its Lord until, in the end, it shall be manifested in full light" (LG 8, 10).

Surrender

The process of discernment can be carried out with great care, be nurtured by wisdom, and lead to clarity about what God is asking. However, none of those important elements of discernment can eliminate the need for us to surrender to God and God's ways as they become evident.

Ignatian Insights

"While he was still in Barcelona before embarking, he sought out, as was his practice, all spiritual persons, even though they lived in hermitages far from the city, to converse with them. But neither in Barcelona nor in Manresa during the whole time he was there did he find persons who could help him as much as he wished; only in Manresa that woman mentioned above, who told him she prayed God that Jesus Christ might appear to him: She alone seemed to him to enter more deeply into spiritual matters. Therefore, after leaving Barcelona, he completely lost this eagerness to seek out spiritual persons" (*Autobiography*, 37).

"The person . . . will benefit greatly . . . by offering all their desires and freedom to him so that His Divine Majesty can make use of their persons and of all they possess in whatsoever way is in accord with his most holy will" (*Spiritual Exercises*, 5).

"The Sixth Point (in making a good and sound election). When that election or decision has been made, the person who has made it ought with great diligence to go to prayer before God our Lord and to offer him that election, that the Divine Majesty may be pleased to receive and confirm it, if it is conducive to his greater service and praise" (*Spiritual Exercises*, 183).

Grace

To surrender with humility and trust to God's mysterious and reconciling ways.

142

"He (Ignatius) received a summons from the Provincial and the Guardian (of the Holy Places). The (Franciscan) Provincial spoke kindly to him, saying that he knew of his good intention to remain in those holy places, and he had given much thought to the matter; but because of the experience he had had with others, he judged that it was not expedient. He (Ignatius) replied to this that he was very firm in his purpose and was resolved . . . to carry it out. . . . If there was nothing binding him under sin, he would not abandon his intention out of any fear. To this the Provincial replied that they had authority from the Apostolic See to have anyone leave the place, or remain there, as they judged, and to excommunicate anyone who was unwilling to obey them; and that in this case they thought that he should not remain, etc. (Ignatius said) in as much as they had so decided with the authority they had, he would obey them" (*Autobiography*, 46–47).

Scripture

"The angel said to her, 'The Holy Spirit will come upon you, and the power of the Most High will overshadow you . . . for nothing will be impossible with God.' Then Mary said, 'Here am I, the servant of the Lord, let it be with me according to your word'" (Luke 1:35, 37–38).

"Then Jesus, crying with a loud voice, said, 'Father, into your hands I commend my spirit.' Having said this, he breathed his last" (Luke 23:46).

"While they were stoning Stephen, he prayed, 'Lord Jesus, receive my spirit'" (Acts 7:59).

Further Resources

John 4:26–30

John 19:30

John 20:27–29

Reflection Questions

CONSIDERATIONS FOR PRAYER

- What thoughts and feeling are evoked in me by the word "surrender"?
- What have been my experiences of surrender throughout my life?
- How peaceful am I when faced with illness or the inevitability of death?
- What image of God helps me at times of surrender?
- What are the interior dispositions that result when I surrender to God?

DISCERNMENT WITHIN A RELATIONSHIP

- Have I learned to distinguish between legitimate invitations to surrender and imposed acts of power which forced me to surrender?
- What happens to my attitude about surrender when I recognize it can be a choice in human freedom?
- Have I enough maturity and interior freedom to be able to yield to others when that is necessary?

DISCERNMENT WITHIN A GROUP

- Do we know when to bring the discussion of a topic to a close?
- Are we able to recognize when God is calling us to let go of even a wonderful dream?

- When I ponder the conditions of the migrating peoples of the world, what happens to my own willingness to surrender more willingly to God?

- When I ponder the causes of violence in the world, what happens to my own willingness to engage in respectful dialogue with those with whom I am in conflict?

Vatican Council II

"From this liberty and docility grows that spiritual insight through which is found a right attitude to the world and to earthly goods" (PO 17, 353).

"The members of each institute should recall, first of all, that when they made profession of the evangelical counsels they were responding to a divine call, to the end that . . . they might live for God alone. They have dedicated their entire lives to God's service . . . [and] to the church's service too" (PC 5, 388–389).

Forgiveness

God's merciful love is the source and model of the grace to reach out in forgiveness. Our human experience will inevitably include times when we are called to forgive those by whom we have been hurt or when we need to ask the forgiveness of others. Without forgiveness, our discernment can be distorted and our moving toward even apparently unrelated decisions can be blocked. Forgiveness, given and received, often brings significant new light and energy to our discernment process.

Ignatian Insights

"Consolation is experienced when the soul sheds tears which move it to love for its Lord—whether they are tears of grief for its own sins, or about the Passion of Christ our Lord, or about other matters directly ordered to his service and praise" (*Spiritual Exercises*, Rules for Discernment, 316).

"I will conclude with a colloquy of mercy—conversing with God our Lord and thanking him for granting me life until now, and proposing, with his grace, amendment for the future. I will conclude by saying the Our Father" (*Spiritual Exercises*, 61).

"The Spaniard with whom he had stayed at the beginning and who had spent his money without paying it back . . . fell sick. While he was thus ill, the pilgrim learned this from a letter of his and felt the desire to visit and help him. He also thought that in those circumstances he could win him over to leave the world and give himself completely to the service of God. In order to achieve this he felt the desire to walk the twenty-eight leagues from Paris to Rouen barefoot, without eating or drinking. As he prayed over this, he felt very afraid. At last he went to St. Dominic's and there he

Grace

To be alert to the gentle urging of the Spirit to accept both God's forgiveness and the forgiveness of others, and to forgive myself and others.

146

decided to go in the manner just mentioned, the great fear he had of tempting God having now passed" (*Autobiography*, 79).

Scripture

"Have mercy on me, O God, according to your steadfast love; according to your abundant mercy blot out my transgressions. Wash me thoroughly from my iniquity, and cleanse me from my sin. Purge me with hyssop, and I shall be clean; wash me, and I shall be whiter than snow. Let me hear joy and gladness; let the bones that you have crushed rejoice. Hide your face from my sins, and blot out all my iniquities" (Psalm 51:1–2, 7–9).

The story of David, Bathsheba, Uriah, Nathan and God's forgiveness (2 Samuel 11:2–12:26).

"Now all the tax collectors and sinners were coming near to listen to him. And the Pharisees and the scribes were grumbling and saying, 'This fellow welcomes sinners and eats with them.' So he told them this parable: 'Which one of you, having a hundred sheep and losing one of them, does not leave the ninety-nine in the wilderness and go after the one that is lost until he finds it? When he has found it, he lays it on his shoulders and rejoices. And when he comes home, he calls together his friends and neighbors, saying to them, 'Rejoice with me, for I have found my sheep that was lost.' Just so, I tell you, there will be more joy in heaven over one sinner who repents than over ninety-nine righteous persons who need no repentance'" (Luke 15:1–7).

"So when you are offering your gift at the altar, if you remember that your brother or sister has something against you, leave your gift there before the altar and go; first be reconciled to your brother or sister, and then come and offer your gift. . . . Give to everyone who begs from you . . . . Love your enemies and pray for those who persecute you. . . . Beware of practicing your piety before others in order to be seen by them. . . . Forgive others their trespasses . . ." (Matthew 5:23–24, 42, 44; 6:1, 14).

Further Resources

2 Samuel 18:33

Genesis 45:4, 5, 8–11

Luke 15:17–24

Romans 2:4

2 Corinthians 5:20–6:2

Reflection Questions

CONSIDERATIONS FOR PRAYER

- Have I learned to rejoice in the mercy of God?

- Is it at times difficult for me to recognize and accept the fact that forgiveness may be lacking in my life?

- Are there persons I need to forgive? Am I forgiving of myself?

- What happens to my prayer when I nurture resentment or anger after a painful experience?

- Do I understand that feelings of hurt may perdure even when forgiveness has been given?

DISCERNMENT WITHIN A RELATIONSHIP

- Are we able to be mutually vulnerable when we need to give or receive forgiveness?

- Have we been faithful to incorporating forgiveness in our relationship?

- Can we reflect together on how moments of forgiveness are helping our relationship to grow?

DISCERNMENT WITHIN A GROUP

- Do we recognize that forgiveness contributes something uniquely valuable to our reviewing and processing our mistakes as a group?

A DISCERNING RELATIONSHIP WITH THE WORLD

- What world issues demonstrate to me that peace can never be lasting without forgiveness?

Vatican Council II

"We must always distinguish between the error (which must always be rejected) and the people in error, who never lose their dignity as persons even though they flounder amid false or inadequate religious ideas. God, who alone is the judge and the searcher of hearts, forbids us to pass judgment on the inner guilt of others. The teaching of Christ even demands that we forgive injury, and the precept of love, which is the commandment of the New Law, includes all our enemies: 'You have heard that it was said, 'You shall love your neighbor and hate your enemy.' But I say to you, love your enemies, do good to them that hate you; and pray for those who persecute and calumniate you' (Mt 5:43–44)" (GS 28, 193–194).

Healing

God's light is healing. It searches out any place within us that awaits the touch of God's grace to make us whole and ready for the new invitation of God that discernment will make evident.

Ignatian Insights

[Ignatius suffered greatly from scruples at Manresa; he was interiorly besieged by different spirits.] "In this way, the Lord deigned that he awake as from sleep. As he now had some experience of the diversity of spirits from the lessons God had given him, he began to examine the means by which that spirit had come. He thus decided with great lucidity not to confess anything from the past any more; and so from that day forward he remained free of those scruples and held it for certain that Our Lord had mercifully deigned to deliver him" (*Autobiography*, 25).

"He got up early the next day, the morning that he was going to set out. As he began to dress, such a great fear came over him that he seemed almost unable to dress himself. In spite of that repugnance he left the house, and the city too, before it was quite daylight. Still the fear was with him constantly and persisted as far as Argenteuil. . . . He passed the town with that spiritual distress, but as he came up to a rise, the thing began to go away. He felt great consolation and spiritual strength, with such joy that he began to shout through the fields and to speak to God, etc." (*Autobiography*, 79).

"Note. This too should be noticed. If such a changeable election was made but not in a sincerely and rightly ordered way, then, if one desires fruits to spring from it which are noteworthy and very pleasing to God our Lord, it is profitable to make it anew in a properly ordered way" (*Spiritual Exercises*, 174).

Grace

To be open to God's healing of any pain or hurt that continues to block my freedom to be available for God's new invitations in my life.

Scripture

"As for me, I said, 'O Lord, be gracious to me; heal me, for I have sinned against you'" (Psalm 41:4).

"Heal me, O Lord, and I shall be healed; save me, and I shall be saved; for you are my praise" (Jeremiah 17:14).

"They brought to him a deaf man who had an impediment in his speech; and they begged him to lay his hand on him. He took him aside in private, away from the crowd, and put his fingers into his ears, and he spat and touched his tongue. Then looking up to heaven, he sighed and said to him, 'Ephphatha,' that is, 'Be opened.' And immediately his ears were opened, his tongue was released, and he spoke plainly. Then Jesus ordered them to tell no one; but the more he ordered them, the more zealously they proclaimed it. They were astounded beyond measure, saying, 'He has done everything well; he even makes the deaf to hear and the mute to speak'" (Mark 7:32–37).

"And ought not this woman, a daughter of Abraham whom Satan bound for eighteen long years, be set free from this bondage on the sabbath day?" (Luke 13:16).

"When he heard that Jesus had come from Judea to Galilee, he went and begged him to come down and heal his son, for he was at the point of death" (John 4:47).

"A leper came to him begging him, and kneeling he said to him, 'If you choose, you can make me clean.' Moved with pity, Jesus stretched out his hand and touched him, and said to him, 'I do choose. Be made clean!'" (Mark 1:40–41).

"By his wounds you have been healed" (1 Peter 2:24).

Further Resources

Psalm 6:2

Jeremiah 3:22

Hosea 6:1

Hosea 14:4

Genesis 45:3–5, 14–15; 46:29–30).

Reflection Questions

CONSIDERATIONS FOR PRAYER

- What periods of my life held particular pain or hurt for me?
- What have I done to open myself to the healing of any painful memories that resulted?
- Are there painful memories that are blocking my freedom now?
- What more can I do in order to become less controlled by that restriction?

DISCERNMENT WITHIN A RELATIONSHIP

- What impact has my personal experience had upon my developing a compassionate stance toward others?
- How have I experienced woundedness as a place of special grace for me and for others?

DISCERNMENT WITHIN A GROUP

- Have we found ways of being a healing presence to one another after experiencing the pain of misunderstanding?

A DISCERNING RELATIONSHIP WITH THE WORLD

- How have my experiences of being healed of physical or emotional pain made me committed to legislation to help people with disabilities or mental illness or chronic medical conditions?

Vatican Council II

"The world which the council has in mind is the world of women and men, the entire human family seen in its total environment. It is the world as the theatre of human history, bearing the marks of its travail, its triumphs and failures. It is the world which Christians believe has been created and is sustained by the love of its maker, has fallen into the slavery of sin but has been freed by Christ, who was crucified and rose again in order to break the stranglehold of the evil one, so that it might be fashioned anew according to God's design and brought to its fulfillment" (GS 2, 164).

". . . Not only does the church communicate divine life to humanity but in a certain sense it casts the reflected light of that divine life over all the earth, notably in the way it heals and elevates the dignity of the human person, in the way it consolidates society, and endows people's daily activity with a deeper sense and meaning. The church, then, believes that through each of its members and its community as a whole it can help to make the human family and its history still more human" (GS 40, 207).

The Discernment Process: Profile of a Discerning Life

. . . for God loves nothing so much as the person who lives with wisdom (Wisdom 7:28).

While there is no one way of living a discerning life, there are people whose life stories reveal what might be called a "profile of a discerning life." For Christians, first among those stories is the story of Jesus. Using discernment as a lens through which to view the life, death, and resurrection of Jesus will always add to one's understanding of response to the Spirit's presence and action. The Emmaus narrative is especially revelatory. These two disciples were taught by God in a very ordinary moment in their lives. The Annunciation narrative captures the wonder and intensity of Mary's being addressed by Gabriel and, to our joy, of her generous faith-response to God.

In our memories of parents, families, friends, mentors, and colleagues, each of us can find persons who have been "bigger than life" for us in their witness of living a discerning life, often at great personal cost. The lives and examples of two holy people have especially given us, the authors, such profiles: St. Ignatius of Loyola (1491–1556), founder of the Society of Jesus, and Venerable Cornelia Connelly (1809–1879), foundress of the Society of the Holy Child Jesus. Each labored in eras and cultures very different from what the world knows in the twenty-first century, but each was able to cut through the complexity and, at times, perversity of his or her situation with a relentless fidelity to God's personal and particular invitations in daily life. Their witness is the occasion of consolation and challenge to us and resulted in rich apostolic fruit for the people of God.

Now it is time for each of you to reflect upon what has become evident to you about discernment and to let that understanding shape your own profile of a discerning life.

Reflection Questions

- Who are models of a discerning life for me? How have they done that?

- What seemed to be the "cost" for them of that faithful discipleship?

- When did I begin to develop a discerning approach in my life?

- What events have called forth aspects of discernment in me?

- What sacrifices do I experience in living a discerning life?

- What satisfactions do I experience in living a discerning life?

- What words capture for me the experience of consolation as I have experienced it?

- What practices help me to stay in consolation?

- What words capture for me the experience of desolation as I have experienced it?

- What experiences make me vulnerable to desolation?

- What additional qualities would I add to this book's presentation of the qualities that lead to a discerning heart and approach to life?

- How do I want to integrate discernment into my daily life and decisions?

Your growing consciousness of discernment can guide you as you move through the Moments of Communion, Commitment, and Mission. Congruence with the qualities found in those moments confirm the authenticity of your discerning ways and refine your appreciation of discernment. Discovering and choosing God's will occasions within you the gifts of compassion, charity, freedom, generosity, peace, joy, hope, decisiveness, and faith. The ways and values of Jesus will become apparent as you work with daily facts to act for justice.

Moment *of* Communion

Mary's Story

Mary said to the angel, "How can this be, since I am a virgin?" The angel said to her, "The Holy Spirit will come upon you, and the power of the Most High will overshadow you; therefore the child to be born will be holy; he will be called Son of God."

~LUKE 1:34–35

The Emmaus Story

As they came near the village to which they were going, he walked ahead as if he were going on. But they urged him strongly, saying, "Stay with us, because it is almost evening and the day is now nearly over." So he went in to stay with them. When he was at the table with them, he took bread, blessed and broke it, and gave it to them. Then their eyes were opened, and they recognized him; and he vanished from their sight.

~LUKE 24:28–31

The Moment of Communion finds us at a deeper level of faith, of interior freedom and of desire to be available for God's plans in our life and relationships. Discernment points our attention toward the qualities of mind, heart and action that reveal the presence and action of God's Spirit within us. Living with the ways and values of Jesus as guide, our choices and decisions must be grounded in compassion, freedom, and generosity, and sustained by hope in God's promises to us.

The Ways and Values of Jesus

As the ways and values of Jesus shape decisions, they also become normative for our decisions. One test of the rightness of a decision is its harmony with gospel values. Loving communion with Jesus is critical at every step in the discernment process.

Ignatian Insights

"The third prelude will be to ask for what I desire. Here it will be to ask for an interior knowledge of Our Lord, who became human for me, that I may love him more intensely and follow him more closely" (*Spiritual Exercises*, 104).

"A colloquy should be made with Our Lady. I beg her to obtain for me grace from her Son and Lord that I may be received under his standard" (*Spiritual Exercises*, 147).

"Those who desire to show greater devotion and to distinguish themselves in total service to their eternal King and universal Lord, will not only offer their persons for the labor, but go further still. They will work against their human sensitivities and against their carnal and worldly love, and they will make offerings of greater worth and moment . . ." (*Spiritual Exercises*, 97).

Scripture

"I came that they may have life, and have it abundantly" (John 10:10).

"You did not choose me but I chose you. And I appointed you to go and bear fruit, fruit that will last, so that the Father will give you whatever you ask him in my name" (John 15:16).

Grace

To deepen my commitment to live faithfully according to the gospel values of Jesus.

"'Do not store up for yourselves treasures on earth. . . . For where your treasure is, there your heart will be also. . . . I tell you, do not worry about your life, what you will eat or what you will drink, or about your body, what you will wear. Is not life more than food, and the body more than clothing? . . . And can any of you by worrying add a single hour to your span of life? . . . Strive first for the kingdom of God and his righteousness, and all these things will be given to you as well. So do not worry about tomorrow. . . . Do not judge, so that you may not be judged . . ." (Matthew 6:19, 21, 25, 27, 33–34; 7:1).

"Then he said to them all, 'If any want to become my followers, let them deny themselves and take up their cross daily and follow me. For those who want to save their life will lose it, and those who lose their life for my sake will save it. What does it profit them if they gain the whole world, but lose or forfeit themselves?'" (Luke 9:23–25).

Reflection Questions

CONSIDERATIONS FOR PRAYER

- What gospel story of Jesus captures for me the invitation to live as Jesus did?

- When have I recognized the distinctively life-giving quality of Jesus' values?

- Which values of Jesus are especially important to me? Which values of Jesus are difficult for me to embrace? Why?

- Am I willing to abandon a path or line of action that reveals itself to be opposed to the values of Jesus?

- Prayerfully consider whether and how "justice is a constitutive element of faith" in my life.

Further Resources

Matthew 5:2–12

Matthew 7:3, 7–8, 12, 28–29

Luke 4:18–19

Luke 19:10

Spiritual Exercises 184

DISCERNMENT WITHIN A RELATIONSHIP ～

- Have I found myself marginalized by others because of my commitment to the person and values of Jesus?
- Which of the values of Jesus are especially important for me to have as part of my relationships?
- Which of Jesus' values do I draw upon most in my relationships?

DISCERNMENT WITHIN A GROUP ～

- What does Jesus' commitment to his disciples say to us about being a group that values collaboration and community?
- In our group interaction, do we act according to the values of Jesus?

A DISCERNING RELATIONSHIP WITH THE WORLD ～

- How do I feel about the growing religious diversity in our nation?
- Which of the values of Jesus do I most want to share with people of other religious traditions?
- What steps am I taking to become more articulate about Christian values so that I can explain them to others who may inquire about my religious tradition?
- How do issues of prejudice and injustice command my attention and move me to action?

"The church, although it needs human resources to carry out its mission, is not set up to seek earthly glory, but to proclaim, and this by its own example, humility and self-denial. Christ was sent by the Father 'to bring good news to the poor . . . to heal the broken hearted'(Lk 4:18), 'to seek and to save what was lost' (Lk 19:10). Similarly, the church encompasses with its love all those who are afflicted by human infirmity and it recognizes in those who are poor and who suffer, the likeness of its poor and suffering founder" (LG 8, 10).

"[There is no basis for any theory or practice which would introduce discrimination between individuals or people with respect to their human dignity or the rights that flow from it.] Therefore, the church reproves, as foreign to the mind of Christ, any discrimination against people or any harassment of them on the basis of their race, color, condition in life or religion" (NA 5, 574).

Compassion

The more that we identify with Jesus, the more we find our heart moved with compassion toward those who struggle in any way. Compassion needs to characterize the consideration of the persons and situations in which we are discerning.

Ignatian Insights

"The plague was then beginning in Paris. . . . The pilgrim chose to enter (a house where someone had the plague). Coming upon a sick person, he comforted him and touched his sore with his hand. After he had comforted and encouraged him a while, he went off alone" (*Autobiography*, 83).

"If the giver of the Exercises sees that the one making them is experiencing desolation and temptation, he or she should not treat that person severely or harshly, but gently and kindly. The director should encourage and strengthen the person for the future, unmask the deceptive tactics of the enemy of our human nature, and help the person to prepare and dispose himself or herself for the consolation which will come" (*Spiritual Exercises*, 7).

"Similarly, this consolation is experienced when the soul sheds tears which move it to love for its Lord—whether they are tears of grief for its own sins, or about the Passion of Christ our Lord, or about other matters directly ordered to his service and praise" (*Spiritual Exercises*, 316).

Grace

To grow in my ability to bring the compassionate ways of Jesus to my judgments about myself, others, and the world.

Scripture

"And I will pour out a spirit of compassion and supplication on the house of David and the inhabitants of Jerusalem, so that, when they look on the one whom they have pierced, they shall mourn for him, as one mourns for an only child, and weep bitterly over him, as one weeps over a firstborn" (Zechariah 12:10).

"When Jesus saw her weeping, and the Jews who came with her also weeping, he was greatly disturbed in spirit and deeply moved. . . . Jesus began to weep. So the Jews said, 'See how he loved him!'" (John 11:33, 35–36).

"A Samaritan while traveling came near [the man who was robbed, stripped, beaten and abandoned half dead]; and when he saw him, he was moved with pity. He went to him and bandaged his wounds, having poured oil and wine on them. Then he put him on his own animal, brought him to an inn, and took care of him. The next day he took out two denarii, gave them to the innkeeper, and said, 'Take care of him; and when I come back, I will repay you whatever more you spend'" (Luke 10:33–35).

"If then there is any encouragement in Christ, any consolation from love, any sharing in the Spirit, any compassion and sympathy, make my joy complete: be of the same mind, having the same love, being in full accord and of one mind" (Philippians 2:1–2).

Reflection Questions

CONSIDERATIONS FOR PRAYER

- How do I respond when I become aware of another's struggle?

- What has helped me to notice God's presence and action in situations of struggle or suffering?

- What helps me to remember that God works through suffering to bring new life?

Further Resources

Luke 9:42

1 Peter 4:14

163

DISCERNMENT WITHIN A RELATIONSHIP ∿

- How does compassion free me to make new choices?
- What effect has receiving another person's compassion had on me?
- Have we learned to be compassionate toward, but not caretakers of, each other?

DISCERNMENT WITHIN A GROUP ∿

- Have we developed a compassionate attitude toward people in situations and institutions whose limits and sinfulness affect us?
- Can we bring compassion to bear in those situations when our decisions are the occasion of pain to others?

A DISCERNING RELATIONSHIP WITH THE WORLD ∿

- How do I resist being unduly influenced by the harshness which is characteristic of much public debate?
- What has my experience of travel contributed to my compassionate and just attitudes toward other people?

"The joys and hopes, the grief and anguish of the people of our time, especially of those who are poor or afflicted, are the joys and hopes, the grief and anguish of the followers of Christ as well. Nothing that is genuinely human fails to find an echo in their hearts" (GS 1, 163).

"Wherever women and men are to be found who are in want of food and drink, of clothing, housing, medicine, work, education, the means necessary for leading a truly human life, wherever there are men and women suffering from misfortune or illness, men and women suffering exile or imprisonment, christian charity should search them out, comfort and care for them and give them the assistance that will relieve their needs. This obligation is especially binding on the more affluent individuals and nations" (AA 8, 414–415).

"The social order requires constant improvement: it must be founded in truth, built on justice, and enlivened by love: it should grow in freedom towards a more humane equilibrium. If these objectives are to be attained there will first have to be a renewal of attitudes and far-reaching social changes" (GS 26, 192).

Charity

A life of charity is the ultimate test of discernment. It will be manifested as we become more and more selfless, faithful, other-directed, respectful, forgiving, patient, just, and caring.

Ignatian Insights

"Finally, under the word consolation I include every increase in hope, faith, and charity, and every interior joy which calls and attracts one toward heavenly things and to the salvation of one's soul, by bringing it tranquility and peace in its Creator and Lord"(*Spiritual Exercises*, Rules for Discernment, 316).

"In this hospice (in Spain in 1535), he began to speak with many who came to visit him, of the things of God, by whose grace much fruit was derived. As soon as he arrived, he decided to teach Christian doctrine every day to children. . . . He also preached . . . with profit and help to the souls who came many miles to hear him. He also made an attempt to eliminate some abuses, and with God's help some were set right, e.g., to have gambling banned under sanction. There was also another abuse there: namely, the girls in that region . . . have become concubines of priests and other men. . . . Much evil results from this custom. The pilgrim persuaded the governor to make a law . . . so this abuse began to be corrected. He got an order to be given that the poor should be provided for officially and regularly" (*Autobiography*, 88–89).

"We may not say anything to harm the reputation of others, defame another or to disparage them" (*Spiritual Exercises*, 41).

Grace

To grow in a mature and steady practice of charity that is selfless, forgiving, and empowering.

"Contemplation to Attain Love, Note: Two preliminary observations should be made. First. Love ought to manifest itself more by deeds than by words. Second. Love consists in a mutual communication. . . . The one who loves gives and communicates to the beloved what he or she has, or a part of what one has or can have; and the beloved in return does the same to the lover" (*Spiritual Exercises*, 230–231).

Scripture

"Beloved, let us love one another, because love is from God; everyone who loves is born of God and knows God. Whoever does not love does not know God, for God is love. God's love was revealed among us in this way: God sent his only Son into the world so that we might live through him. In this is love, not that we loved God but that he loved us and sent his Son to be the atoning sacrifice for our sins. Beloved, since God loved us so much, we also ought to love one another. No one has ever seen God; if we love one another, God lives in us, and his love is perfected in us"(1 John 4:7–12).

"Let love be genuine; hate what is evil, hold fast to what is good; love one another with mutual affection" (Romans 12:9–10).

"If I speak in the tongues of mortals and of angels, but do not have love, I am a noisy gong or a clanging cymbal. And if I have prophetic powers, and understand all mysteries and all knowledge, and if I have all faith, so as to remove mountains, but do not have love, I am nothing. If I give away all my possessions, and if I hand over my body so that I may boast, but do not have love, I gain nothing. Love is patient; love is kind; love is not envious or boastful or arrogant. Love never ends. But as for prophecies, they will come to an end; as for tongues, they will cease; as for knowledge, it will come to an end. And now faith, hope, and love abide, these three; and the greatest of these is love" (1 Corinthians 13:1–4, 8, 13).

Further Resources

John 15:9–11

John 13:35

Matthew 5:44, 46

Luke 7:47

1 John 4:18–21

Ephesians 3:17, 19

Reflection Questions

CONSIDERATIONS FOR PRAYER

- When have I had an experience of God's love moving within me?
- Do I recognize my experience of "any increase of love" as consolation?
- When I am moved by a desire to respond to God's love, how does my love for God and others change?
- What have I noticed about how my love for God has been purified?

DISCERNMENT WITHIN A RELATIONSHIP

- Which relationships in my life have been most shaped by an awareness of God's love for us?
- Has my experience of being loved by others helped me to become more generous in loving others?
- What effect does selfishness have upon my relationships with others?
- In which relationships am I most challenged to love as Christ did?

DISCERNMENT WITHIN A GROUP

- If there is a legitimate reason for our group to discuss others, is our conversation marked by charity?
- Are we charitable to each other even when we are in conflict?
- What are the signs of growth in charity in our group?

A DISCERNING RELATIONSHIP WITH THE WORLD

- What changes in my way of loving the world result from a consideration of the profound interconnectedness of all things in creation?
- What are my responses when I learn about people entering danger to help another?

"It is therefore quite clear that all Christians in whatever state or walk of life are called to the fullness of Christian life and to the perfection of charity, and this holiness is conducive to a more human way of living. . ." (LG 40, 59–60).

"Christian charity is extended to all without distinction of race, social condition, or religion, and seeks neither gain nor gratitude. Just as God loves us with a gratuitous love, so too the faithful, in their charity, should be concerned for people, loving them with that same love with which God sought out humanity. As Christ went about all the towns and villages healing every sickness and infirmity . . . so the church . . . joins itself with people of every condition, but especially with the poor and afflicted, and willingly spends itself for them" (Decree on the Church's Missionary Activity, AGD 12, 459).

"Works of charity and mercy bear a most striking testimony to Christian life. . . . The performance of these works should enable the faithful to learn from childhood how to sympathize with their brothers and sisters, and help them generously when in need" (AA 31, 440).

"In our day, when people are drawing more closely together and the bonds of friendship between different peoples are being strengthened, the church examines more carefully its relations with non-christian religions. Ever aware of its duty to foster unity and charity among individuals, and even among nations, it reflects at the outset on what people have in common and what tends to bring them together" (NA 1, 569).

Freedom

· · · · · · · · ·

A faith-filled discernment leads to ever-deepening interior freedom. New areas of unfreedom will continually come to our attention. Each awareness will draw us into the life-giving dynamic of Jesus' death-resurrection which truly frees us.

Ignatian Insights

"Accordingly, one . . . ought not to lean or incline in either direction but rather, while standing by like the pointer of a scale in equilibrium, to allow the Creator to deal immediately with the creature and the creature with its Creator and Lord" (*Spiritual Exercises*, 15).

"For this purpose—namely, that the Creator and Lord may with greater certainty be the one working in his creature—if by chance the [person] feels an affection or inclination to something in a disordered way, it is profitable for that person to strive with all possible effort to come over to the opposite of that to which he or she is wrongly attached. Thus, if someone is inclined to pursue and hold on to an office . . . not for the honor and glory of God our Lord or for the spiritual welfare of souls, but rather for one's own temporal advantages and interests, one should try to bring oneself to desire the opposite. One should make earnest prayers and other Spiritual Exercises, and ask God our Lord for the contrary; that is, to have no desire for this . . . or anything else unless the Divine Majesty has put proper order into those desires, and has by this means so changed one's earlier attachment that one's motive in desiring or holding on to one thing rather than another will now be only the service, honor, and glory of the Divine Majesty" (*Spiritual Exercises*, 16).

Grace

To choose those options that will help me to grow in greater freedom from the attachments, biases, and preferences that block my availability for God's action in my life.

Scripture

"Then Jesus said to the Jews who had believed in him, 'If you continue in my word, you are truly my disciples; and you will know the truth, and the truth will make you free. . . . So if the Son makes you free, you will be free indeed'" (John 8:31–32, 36).

"He himself bore our sins in his body on the cross, so that, free from sins, we might live for righteousness; by his wounds you have been healed" (1 Peter 2:24).

"Creation itself will be set free from its bondage to decay and will obtain the freedom of the glory of the children of God" (Romans 8:21).

"Now the Lord is the Spirit, and where the Spirit of the Lord is, there is freedom" (2 Corinthians 3:17).

"For freedom Christ has set us free. Stand firm, therefore, and do not submit again to a yoke of slavery. . . . For you were called to freedom, brothers and sisters; only do not use your freedom as an opportunity for self-indulgence . . ." (Galatians 5:1, 13).

Reflection Questions

CONSIDERATIONS FOR PRAYER

- What are signs to me that I am acting with interior freedom?
- What are signs that I am not interiorly free?
- In what areas of my life do I need to become more free and trusting of God?
- What is my experience of using the power I have, whether because of my education, age, income, or networking?

Further Resources

Galatians 1:3–4
1 Peter 2:16

- Can I remember and draw on memories of times when I was free enough to open myself completely to God's presence and action?
- What scripture figures give me hope of becoming more free?

DISCERNMENT WITHIN A RELATIONSHIP ∿

- What happens in my relationships when I bring interior freedom to the interactions?
- What can I bring to my relationships that will encourage others to act with interior freedom?
- What are the signs to me that my lack of freedom is "hooked" to another's lack of freedom? Am I free enough to address this with the other person?
- How have I learned not to be controlled by others' expectations of me?
- Do I have a realistic awareness of my own needs? When appropriate, can I present them to others while leaving them free to respond or not?
- Are we using our power in healthy ways with each other?
- If considering marriage or a vowed life, what are the signs that I am free to make that commitment?

DISCERNMENT WITHIN A GROUP ∿

- Is a spirit of trusting freedom permeating our interactions?
- Are we using power in ways that free and enhance rather than bind or exclude?

A DISCERNING RELATIONSHIP WITH THE WORLD ∿

- What situations make me aware of the difference between true freedom and selfish license?
- What freedom does my economic situation give me? What are the corresponding responsibilities that I have?

"The church has been sent to all ages and nations and, therefore, is not tied exclusively and indissolubly to any race or nation, to any one particular way of life, or to any set of customs, ancient or modern. The church is faithful to its traditions and is at the same time conscious of its universal mission; it can, then, enter into communion with different forms of culture, thereby enriching both itself and the cultures themselves. . . . In this way the church carries out its mission and in that very act it stimulates and advances human and civil culture, as well as contributing by its activity, including liturgical activity, to humanity's interior freedom" (GS 58, 234–235).

"Furthermore, since civil society has the right to protect itself against possible abuses committed in the name of religious freedom, the responsibility of providing such protection rests especially with the civil authority. However, this must not be done in an arbitrary manner or by the unfair practice of favoritism but in accordance with legal principles which are in conformity with the objective moral order. These principles are necessary for the effective protection of the rights of all citizens and for the peaceful settlement of conflicts of rights. They are also necessary for an adequate protection of that just public peace which is to be found where people live together in good order and true justice. They are required too for the necessary protection of public morality" (DH 7, 558).

Generosity

God's grace may empower us to act with more generosity than we ever dreamed would be possible when responding alone.

Ignatian Insights

"I will call back into my memory the gifts I have received—my creation, redemption, and other gifts particular to myself. I will ponder with deep affection how much God our Lord has done for me, and how much he has given me of what he possesses . . . even his very self . . ." (*Spiritual Exercises*, 234).

"One day . . . a beggar asked him for alms and he gave him a *marchetto*, which is a coin of five or six *quatrini*. After that another came, and he gave him another small coin that he had, somewhat larger; and to a third he gave a *giulio*, having nothing but *giulii*. The beggars, seeing that he was giving alms, kept coming and so all he had was finished. Finally, many beggars came together seeking alms. His response was to ask pardon, as he had nothing left" (*Autobiography*, 50).

"Colloquy. Imagine Christ our Lord suspended on the cross before you, and converse with him in a colloquy: 'How is it that he, although he is the Creator, has come to make himself a human being? How is it that he has passed from eternal life to death here in time, and to die in this way for my sins?' In a similar way, reflect on yourself and ask: 'What have I done for Christ? What am I doing for Christ? What ought I to do for Christ?' In this way, too, gazing on him in so pitiful a state as he hangs on the cross, speak out whatever comes to your mind" (*Spiritual Exercises*, 53).

Grace

To be generous in my response to God's invitations whether they come in prayer, relationships, groups, or in the needs of the world.

"Those who desire to show greater devotion and to distinguish themselves in total service to their eternal King and universal Lord, will not only offer their persons for the labor, but go further still. They will work against their human sensitivities and against their carnal and worldly love, and they will make offerings of greater worth and moment" (*Spiritual Exercises*, 97).

Scripture

"Take what belongs to you and go; I choose to give to this last the same as I give to you. Am I not allowed to do what I choose with what belongs to me? Or are you envious because I am generous?" (Matthew 20:14–15).

"For there is no distinction between Jew and Greek; the same Lord is Lord of all and is generous to all who call on him" (Romans 10:12).

"For you know the generous act of our Lord Jesus Christ, that though he was rich, yet for your sakes he became poor, so that by his poverty you might become rich" (2 Corinthians 8:9).

"You will be enriched in every way for your great generosity, which will produce thanksgiving to God through us. . . . Through the testing of this ministry you glorify God by your obedience to the confession of the gospel of Christ and by the generosity of your sharing with them and with all others" (2 Corinthians 9:11, 13).

"By contrast, the fruit of the Spirit is love, joy, peace, patience, kindness, generosity, faithfulness" (Galatians 5:22).

Further Resources

Acts 4:32–35

James 1:17

Ephesians 2:4

Romans 12:6–8

GS 85, 272–273

Reflection Questions

CONSIDERATIONS FOR PRAYER

- What experiences have formed a generous spirit in me?
- Who are the people who have modeled generosity for me?
- In what concrete ways do I practice generosity with my time, my presence, my expertise?
- In what ways have I learned to counter the individualistic spirit that can surround me?
- What do I do with the fear that can get in the way of a generous response?

DISCERNMENT WITHIN A RELATIONSHIP

- What are the ways I bring generosity to our relationship?
- Am I willing to be generous when another cannot respond with generosity or appreciation?

DISCERNMENT WITHIN A GROUP

- Have we learned the difference between being generous and responding to manipulation or unreasonable expectations from within or from outside the group?
- Are we generous with our time, expertise, and attitudes?

A DISCERNING RELATIONSHIP WITH THE WORLD

- What are my honest thoughts and feelings about programs that call for my generosity?
- What is my motivation for being generous in giving to those in need?

"In their pilgrimage . . . Christians are to seek and value the things that are above; this involves not less, but greater commitment to working with everyone for the establishment of a more human world. Indeed, the mystery of their faith provides Christians with greater incentive and encouragement to fulfill their role more willingly and to assess the significance of activities capable of assigning to human culture its honored role in the complete vocation of humanity" (GS 57, 232).

"A life like this calls for a continuous exercise of faith, hope and charity. Only the light of faith and meditation on the word of God can enable us to find everywhere and always the God 'in whom we live and exist" (Acts 17:28); only thus can we seek his will in everything, see Christ in everyone, acquaintance or stranger, make sound judgments on the true meaning and value of temporal realities both in themselves and in relation to our final end" (AA 4, 408).

Moment *of* Commitment

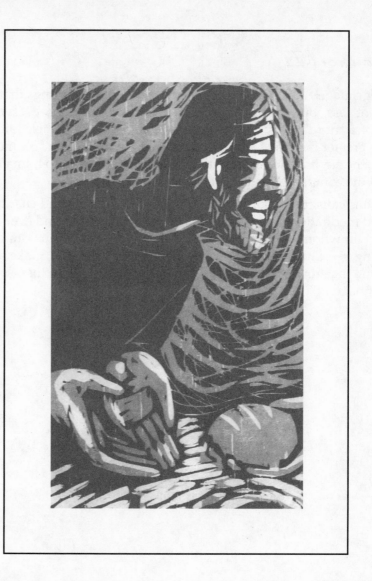

Mary's Story

"And now, your relative Elizabeth in her old age has also conceived a son; and this is the sixth month for her who was said to be barren. For nothing will be impossible with God." Then Mary said, "Here am I, the servant of the Lord; let it be with me according to your word." Then the angel departed from her.

~Luke 1:36–38

The Emmaus Story

They said to each other, "Were not our hearts burning within us while he was talking to us on the road, while he was opening the scriptures to us?" That same hour they got up and returned to Jerusalem.

~Luke 24:32–33

The active impulse of the Spirit will move us to commitment, that loving choice which gives solid expression to who we are becoming as disciples of Jesus. Attention to the interior love, peace and joy which are the gifts of the Spirit takes us to a new clarity about God's will for us. Bringing a discerning heart to the decisions of ordinary days strengthens our hope that God will make us ready to engage in a process of discernment when faced with a significant decision.

Peace

· · · · · ·

Especially at times of discernment, one looks for that quality of peace which is the unfailing sign of being united with God and God's designs. In discernment, one must also be alert to the possibility of a false peace which can at times harbor one's resistance to or denial of God's invitations and action.

Ignatian Insights

"In the case of those who are going from good to better, the good angel touches the soul gently, lightly, and sweetly, like a drop of water going into a sponge. The evil spirit touches it sharply, with noise and disturbance, like a drop of water falling onto a stone. In the case of those who are going from bad to worse, these spirits touch the souls in the opposite manner. The reason for this is the fact that the disposition of the soul is either similar to or different from the respective spirits who are entering. When the soul is different, they enter with perceptible noise and are quickly noticed. When the soul is similar, they enter silently, like those who go into their own house by an open door" (*Spiritual Exercises*, Rules for Discernment, 335).

"For what fills and satisfies the soul consists, not in knowing much, but in our understanding the realities profoundly and in savoring them interiorly" (*Spiritual Exercises*, 2).

"While he was there (Chioggia), Christ appeared to him in the manner in which he usually appeared to him . . . and this brought him much comfort" (*Autobiography*, 41).

"He maintained himself in Venice by begging, and he slept in St. Mark's Square. . . . He had a great assurance in his soul that God would provide a way for him to go to

Grace

To recognize and reverence the peace that fills me when I am living in ways that are in harmony with God's desires.

180

Jerusalem; this gave him such confidence that no arguments or fears suggested to him could make him doubt" (*Autobiography*, 42).

Scripture

"May the Lord give strength to his people! May the Lord bless his people with peace!" (Psalm 29:11).

"For he is our peace; in his flesh he has made both groups into one and has broken down the dividing wall, that is, the hostility between us. He has abolished the law with its commandments and ordinances, that he might create in himself one new humanity in place of the two, thus making peace. . . . So he came and proclaimed peace to you who were far off and peace to those who were near" (Ephesians 2:14–15, 17).

"If you had walked in the way of God, you would be living in peace forever. Learn where there is wisdom, where there is strength, where there is understanding, so that you may at the same time discern where there is length of days, and life, where there is light for the eyes, and peace" (Baruch 3:13–14).

"And the peace of God, which surpasses all understanding, will guard your hearts and your minds in Christ Jesus. Keep on doing the things that you have learned and received and heard and seen in me, and the God of peace will be with you" (Philippians 4:7, 19).

"Peace I leave with you; my peace I give to you. I do not give to you as the world gives. Do not let your hearts be troubled, and do not let them be afraid" (John 14:27).

"Let us then pursue what makes for peace and for mutual upbuilding" (Romans 14:19).

Further Resources

Isaiah 55:7, 12

Luke 10:5–6

Colossians 3:15–17

Matthew 5:9

Reflection Questions

CONSIDERATIONS FOR PRAYER

- What are the signs to me that I am at peace? Not at peace?

- What do I typically do when I am at war within myself?

- What helps me to recognize my need to address the cause of not being at peace?

- Have I ever had an experience in prayer in which I came to peace about something?

- What do I remember about that experience?

DISCERNMENT WITHIN A RELATIONSHIP

- Am I willing to accept what interior peace or its absence may be revealing to me about my relationships?

- What effect do stress and anxiety have on my relationships?

- What helps me to remain peaceful in situations of stress?

DISCERNMENT WITHIN A GROUP

- When has our group experienced moving through struggle to peace?

- Are we alert to the possibility of being lulled into a false sense of peace by denial of something that needs attention among us?

A DISCERNING RELATIONSHIP WITH THE WORLD

- What do I do when my personal inner peace is disturbed by the lack of peace in the world?

- Which world, national, or church figures have modeled peacemaking in ways that inspire me?

"In our generation, which has been marked by the persistent and severe hardships and anxiety resulting from the ravages of war and the threat of war, the whole human race faces a moment of supreme crisis in its advance towards maturity. Humanity has gradually come closer together and is everywhere more conscious of its own unity; but it will not succeed in accomplishing the task awaiting it, that is, the establishment of a truly human world for all over the entire earth, unless all devote themselves to the cause of true peace with renewed vigor. Thus the message of the Gospel, which epitomizes the highest ideals and aspirations of humanity, throws a new light in our times when it proclaims that the advocates of peace are blessed 'for they shall be called children of God' (Mt 5:9)" (GS 77, 262–263).

"Peace cannot be achieved . . . unless people's welfare is safeguarded and people freely and in a spirit of mutual trust share with one another the riches of their minds and their talents. A firm determination to respect the dignity of other individuals and peoples along with the deliberate practice of friendliness are absolutely necessary for the achievement of peace. Accordingly, peace is also the fruit of love, for love goes beyond what justice can achieve" (GS 78, 263–264).

Joy

• • • •

Joy, a gift of God's Spirit, is the fruit of God's love within a person. It is a sign of consolation and can coexist with the suffering or challenge that are aspects of any commitment.

Ignatian Insights

"Finally, under the word consolation I include every increase in . . . interior joy which calls and attracts one toward heavenly things and to the salvation of one's soul, by bringing it tranquility and peace in its Creator and Lord" (*Spiritual Exercises,* Rules for Discernment, 316).

"The First Rule. It is characteristic of God and his angels, by the motions they cause, to give genuine happiness and spiritual joy, and thereby to banish any sadness and turmoil induced by the enemy. It is characteristic of the enemy to fight against this happiness and spiritual consolation, by using specious reasonings, subtleties, and persistent deceits" (*Spiritual Exercises,* Rules for Discernment, 329).

"During this period our Lord appeared to him (Ignatius) on many occasions, giving him much strength and consolation. . . . [When] making their way to Jerusalem . . . when the pilgrim did see the city, he experienced great consolation, and all the others affirmed the same, saying that they all felt a joy that did not seem natural. He felt this same devotion on all his visits to the Holy Places" (*Autobiography,* 44).

"Another time, in the year fifty, he was very bad with a severe illness which, in his opinion as well as of many others, would be the last. On this occasion, thinking about death, he felt such joy and such spiritual consolation at having to die that he dissolved entirely into tears. This became so habitual that he often stopped thinking about death so as not to feel so much of that consolation" (*Autobiography,* 33).

Grace

To rejoice in the awareness that God acts within me and in my life situation.

Scripture

"Sing for joy, O heavens, and exult, O earth; break forth, O mountains, into singing! For the LORD has comforted his people, and will have compassion on his suffering ones" (Isaiah 49:13).

"I will turn their mourning into joy, I will comfort them, and give them gladness for sorrow" (Jeremiah 31:13).

"As soon as I heard the sound of your greeting, the child in my womb leaped for joy" (Luke 1:44).

"The kingdom of heaven is like treasure hidden in a field, which someone found and hid; then in his joy he goes and sells all that he has and buys that field" (Matthew 13:44).

"I tell you, there will be more joy in heaven over one sinner who repents than over ninety-nine righteous persons who need no repentance" (Luke 15:7).

"Very truly, I tell you, you will weep and mourn, but the world will rejoice; you will have pain, but your pain will turn into joy. . . . So you have pain now; but I will see you again, and your hearts will rejoice, and no one will take your joy from you. . . . Until now you have not asked for anything in my name. Ask and you will receive, so that your joy may be complete" (John 16:20, 22, 24).

"Looking to Jesus the pioneer and perfecter of our faith, who for the sake of the joy that was set before him endured the cross . . ." (Hebrews 12:2).

"Although you have not seen him, you love him; and even though you do not see him now, you believe in him and rejoice with an indescribable and glorious joy" (1 Peter 1:8).

"May the God of hope fill you with all joy and peace in believing, so that you may abound in hope by the power of the Holy Spirit" (Romans 15:13).

Further Resources

Psalm 5:11

John 15:11

John 17:13

Acts 13:52

Galatians 5:22

1 Thessalonians 1:6

Reflection Questions

CONSIDERATIONS FOR PRAYER

- Do I turn to God when I am joyful?
- Have I ever experienced joy and sorrow or pain at the same time?
- By distinguishing among the various feelings occasioned by a particular event, do I ever discover both consolation and desolation in an experience?
- Do I pray for joy for myself and others?

DISCERNMENT WITHIN A RELATIONSHIP

- What are some of the ways in which I find joy in my relationships?
- Can I distinguish between having fun and being joyful?

DISCERNMENT WITHIN A GROUP

- Do we support others when they are rejoicing?
- How do we respond when we are experiencing both joy and sorrow in the group?

A DISCERNING RELATIONSHIP WITH THE WORLD

- Which entertainments and forms of relaxation lead me to true joy?
- Is the generosity and talent of scientists in their efforts to help humanity an occasion of joy for me?

"The Word of God, through whom all things were made, was made flesh, so that as a perfect man he could save all women and men and sum up all things in himself. The Lord is the goal of human history, the focal point of the desires of history and civilization, the center of humanity, the joy of all hearts, and the fulfillment of all aspirations" (GS 45, 216).

"Let married people themselves, who are created in the image of the living God and constituted in an authentic personal dignity, be united together in equal affection, agreement of mind and mutual holiness. Thus, in the footsteps of Christ, the principle of life, they will bear witness by their faithful love in the joys and sacrifices of their calling, to that mystery of love which the Lord revealed to the world by his death and resurrection" (GS 52, 227–228).

Hope

Discerning God's will places our hope squarely in God's promise to be with us always. Hope empowers us to move patiently through the various steps of a discernment process with confidence that the will of God will become clear.

Ignatian Insights

"They boarded the pilgrim ship, on which also he brought no more for his maintenance than his hope in God" (*Autobiography*, 44).

"So at the beginning of the year '23 he set out for Barcelona to take ship. Although there were some offers of company, he wanted to go quite alone, for his whole idea was to have God alone as refuge. . . . He wanted to practice three virtues—charity, faith, and hope. If he took a companion, he would expect help from him when he was hungry; if he fell down, the man would help him get up; and so also he would trust him and feel attachment to him on this account; but he wanted to place that trust, attachment and expectation in God alone" (*Autobiography*, 35).

"I will consider how God labors and works for me in all creatures on the face of the earth; that is, he acts in the manner of one who is laboring. . . . Working in the heavens, elements, plants, fruits, cattle, and all the rest—giving them their existence, conserving them, concurring with their vegetative and sensitive activities, and so forth" (*Spiritual Exercises*, 236).

"Finally, under the word consolation I include every increase in hope . . . which calls and attracts one toward heavenly things and to the salvation of one's soul, by bringing it tranquility and peace in its Creator and Lord" (*Spiritual Exercises*, Rules for Discernment, 316).

Grace

To open myself to the outpouring of God's Spirit that will confirm my hope.

"The Fourth Rule. Imagining and considering how I will find myself on judgment day, I will think how at that time I will wish I had decided in regard to the present matter. And the rule which I will then wish I had followed is what I shall apply now, in order that then I may be in complete contentment and joy" (*Spiritual Exercises*, 187).

Scripture

"For God alone my soul waits in silence, for my hope is from him" (Psalm 62:5).

"I will wait for the LORD, who is hiding his face . . . and I will hope in him" (Isaiah 8:17).

"I know the plans I have for you . . . plans for your welfare and not for harm, to give you a future with hope. Then when you call upon me and come and pray to me, I will hear you. When you search for me, you will find me; if you seek me with all your heart, I will let you find me" (Jeremiah 29:11–13).

"But this I call to mind, and therefore I have hope: The steadfast love of the LORD never ceases, his mercies never come to an end; they are new every morning; great is your faithfulness. 'The LORD is my portion,' says my soul, 'therefore I will hope in him.' The LORD is good to those who wait for him, to the soul that seeks him. It is good that one should wait quietly for the salvation of the LORD" (Lamentations 3:21–26).

"Endurance produces character, and character produces hope, and hope does not disappoint us, because God's love has been poured into our hearts through the Holy Spirit that has been given to us" (Romans 5:4–5).

"For in hope we were saved. Now hope that is seen is not hope. For who hopes for what is seen? But if we hope for what we do not see, we wait for it with patience" (Romans 8:24–25).

"With the eyes of your heart enlightened, you may know what is the hope to which he has called you . . ." (Ephesians 1:18).

Further Resources

Sirach 11:21

1 Peter 1:21

Romans 12:12

Romans 15:13

Hebrews 6:19

Hebrews 10:23

1 Peter 1:3

Gaudium et spes, 23

Reflection Questions

CONSIDERATIONS FOR PRAYER

- When have I had to wait in hope?
- What gives me hope on a daily basis?
- How has my hope been attacked by discouragement or despair?
- Have I learned the difference between hope and optimism?

DISCERNMENT WITHIN A RELATIONSHIP

- Are my relationships characterized by hope or by cynicism?
- Do I bring to others a hope that I and they can change and grow?
- In what settings do I find it difficult to be hopeful? What is this telling me?

DISCERNMENT WITHIN A GROUP

- In what areas are there still challenges before us?
- Are we grounding ourselves in hope as we prepare to address them?

A DISCERNING RELATIONSHIP WITH THE WORLD

- In what ways do the world's children both give me hope and challenge my responsibility to give them a hopeful future?

"This synod wishes to set forth the authentic teaching on divine revelation and its transmission. For it wants the whole world to hear the summons to salvation, so that through hearing it may believe, through belief it may hope, through hope it may come to love" (DV 1, 97).

"Great numbers of people are acutely conscious of being deprived of the world's goods through injustice and unfair distribution and are vehemently demanding their share of them. Developing nations . . . are anxious to share in the political and economic benefits of modern civilization and to play their part freely in the world, but they are hampered by their economic dependence on the rapidly expanding richer nations and the ever-widening gap between them. The hungry nations cry out to their affluent neighbors; women claim parity with men in fact as well as of right. . . . Now for the first time in history people are not afraid to think that cultural benefits are for all and should be available to everybody. These claims are but the sign of a deeper and more widespread aspiration. Women and men as individuals and as members of society crave a life that is full, autonomous, and worthy of their nature as human beings; they long to harness for their own welfare the immense resources of the modern world. Among nations there is a growing movement to set up a worldwide community" (GS 9, 170–171).

Decisiveness

Discernment is intended to lead to free choices and decisions. Personal choices are fragile human acts leading to decisions that can be powerful in their consequences for ourselves and others. God's steadfast fidelity to us is the source of our confidence in making those discerned decisions.

Ignatian Insights

"The desire to be able to serve God our Lord better is what moves one to take or reject any object whatsoever" (*Spiritual Exercises*, 155).

"The Fourth Rule. It is characteristic of the evil angel, who takes on the appearance of an angel of light, to enter by going along the same way as the devout soul and then to exit by his own way with success for himself. That is, he brings good and holy thoughts attractive to such an upright soul and then strives little by little to get his own way, by enticing the soul over to his own hidden deceits and evil intentions" (*Spiritual Exercises*, Rules for Discernment, 332).

"During a time of desolation one should never make a change. Instead, one should remain firm and constant in the resolutions and in the decision which one had on the day before the desolation, or in a decision in which one was during a previous time of consolation. For just as the good spirit is chiefly the one who guides and counsels us in time of consolation, so it is the evil spirit who does this in time of desolation. By following his counsels we can never find the way to a right decision" (*Spiritual Exercises*, Rules for Discernment, 318).

Grace

To accept the significance and consequences of decisions in my life.

"There are three chief causes for the desolation in which we find ourselves.

"The first is that we ourselves are tepid, lazy, or negligent in our spiritual exercises. The second is that the desolation is meant to test how much we are worth and how far we will extend ourselves in the service and praise of God, even without much repayment by way of consolations and increased graces. The third is that the desolation is meant to give us a true recognition and understanding, so that we may perceive interiorly that we cannot by ourselves bring on or retain great devotion, intense love, tears, or any other spiritual consolation, but that all these are a gift and grace from God our Lord. . . . (*Spiritual Exercises*, Rules for Discernment, 322).

Scripture

"I call heaven and earth to witness against you today that I have set before you life and death, blessings and curses. Choose life so that you and your descendants may live" (Deuteronomy 30:19).

"A leper came to him begging him, and kneeling he said to him, 'If you choose, you can make me clean.' Moved with pity, Jesus stretched out his hand and touched him, and said to him, 'I do choose. Be made clean!'" (Mark 1:40–41).

"The young man said to him, 'I have kept all these; what do I still lack?' Jesus said to him, 'If you wish to be perfect, go, sell your possessions, and give the money to the poor, and you will have treasure in heaven; then come, follow me.' When the young man heard this word, he went away grieving, for he had many possessions" (Matthew 19:20–22).

"You did not choose me but I chose you. And I appointed you to go and bear fruit, fruit that will last, so that the Father will give you whatever you ask him in my name" (John 15:16).

Further Resources

Sirach 15:15

Job 34:4

Isaiah 58:6

Deuteronomy 1:13

1 Corinthians 3:10

Spiritual Exercises 21, 46

Diguitatis Hamanae 3, 554

Reflection Questions

CONSIDERATIONS FOR PRAYER

- What indicates to me that it is time to make a decision?

- Have I ever felt the burden of having to make a very difficult decision?

- What have been the ways in which I have used my gifts and freedom for good decisions? For poor decisions?

- Do I prayerfully consider my motivation before making decisions?

- What prevents me from making good decisions and acting upon them?

- Have I developed a habit of praying about my decisions?

DISCERNMENT WITHIN A RELATIONSHIP

- Does the relationship allow for my good decisions? For the other's good decisions?

- Am I open to finding new ways of strengthening our relationship?

- Do I, at times, make unwarranted assumptions about another's decisions?

- In what circumstances do I tend to surrender to others my responsibility to decide?

- What is imposing real limits upon our decisions in the relationship at this time?

DISCERNMENT WITHIN A GROUP

- What decisions will we need to make in the next six months?

- Will it be appropriate to use discernment as the process for coming to the decision? If not, what method will we use?

- Am I willing to trust and accept the decision of the group?

- How have my decisions been simplified or complicated by globalization and the developments in technology?

- Am I becoming more decisive regarding justice issues and concerns?

Vatican Council II

"The fact that human beings are social by nature indicates that the betterment of the person and the improvement of society depend on each other. Insofar as humanity by its very nature stands completely in need of life in society, it is and it ought to be the beginning, the subject and the object of every social organization. Life in society is not something accessory to humanity: through their dealings with others, through mutual service, and through . . . dialogue, men and women develop all their talents and become able to rise to their destiny" (GS 25, 190).

"Because of the increasingly close interdependence which is gradually extending to the entire world, we are today witnessing an extension of the role of the common good, which is the sum total of social conditions which allow people, either as groups or as individuals, to reach their fulfillment more fully and more easily. The resulting rights and obligations are consequently the concern of the entire human race. Every group must take into account the needs and legitimate aspirations of every other group, and even those of the human family as a whole. At the same time, however, there is a growing awareness of the sublime dignity of human persons, who stand above all things and whose rights and duties are universal and inviolable. They ought . . . to have ready access to all that is necessary for living a genuinely human life: for example, food, clothing, housing, the right freely to choose their state of life and set up a family, the right to education, work, to their good name, to respect, to proper knowledge, the right to act according to the dictates of conscience and to safeguard their privacy, and rightful freedom, including freedom of religion" (GS 26, 191).

Moment of Mission

Mary's Story

In those days Mary set out and went with haste to a Judean town in the hill country, where she entered the house of Zechariah and greeted Elizabeth. When Elizabeth heard Mary's greeting, the child leaped in her womb. And Elizabeth was filled with the Holy Spirit and exclaimed with a loud cry, "Blessed are you among women, and blessed is the fruit of your womb. And why has this happened to me, that the mother of my Lord comes to me? For as soon as I heard the sound of your greeting, the child in my womb leaped for joy. And blessed is she who believed that there would be a fulfillment of what was spoken to her by the Lord." And Mary said, "My soul magnifies the Lord, and my spirit rejoices in God my Savior, for he has looked with favor on the lowliness of his servant. Surely, from now on all generations will call me blessed; for the Mighty One has done great things for me, and holy is his name."

~LUKE 1:39–49

The Emmaus Story

They found the eleven and their companions gathered together. They were saying, "The Lord has risen indeed, and he has appeared to Simon!" Then they told what had happened on the road, and how he had been made known to them in the breaking of the bread.

~LUKE 24:33–35

In the Moment of Mission, we discover that we have become persons who have been radically changed and have turned from living according to our own will and wisdom. God's will and wisdom is manifested now by the Spirit at work in the minds and hearts of believers. Faith and trust in God's loving will for the world grounds our confidence as we discern the actions for justice to which the Spirit leads us.

Faith

Discernment builds upon the belief that a provident God guides our lives. Discernment provides a faith-based way of making decisions that are in harmony with God's desires for the world and for ourselves. Having discerned a decision, we must implement it in faith.

Ignatian Insights

"On the way [to Montserrat] something happened to him which it would be well to record, so one may understand how Our Lord dealt with this soul, which was still blind, though greatly desirous of serving him as far as his knowledge went. . . . From . . . [his desire to please and gratify God] he derived all his consolation. . . . His whole intention was to do such great external works because the saints had done so for the glory of God, without considering any more particular prospect" (*Autobiography*, 14).

"Once, the manner in which God had created the world was presented to his understanding with great spiritual joy. . . . Often and for a long time, while at prayer, he saw with interior eyes the humanity of Christ. . . . He has also seen Our Lady in a similar form. . . . These things he saw strengthened him then and always gave him such strength in his faith that he has often thought to himself: if there were no Scriptures to teach us these matters of faith, he would be resolved to die for them, solely because of what he has seen" (*Autobiography*, 29).

The First Time is an occasion when God our Lord moves and attracts the will in such a way that a devout person, without doubting or being able to doubt, carries out what was proposed" (*Spiritual Exercises*, 175).

Grace

To continue to place my faith in God who has created, redeemed, and sanctified me through the life-death-resurrection of Jesus Christ.

"Finally, under the word consolation I include every increase in . . . faith . . . which calls and attracts one toward heavenly things and to the salvation of one's soul, by bringing it tranquility and peace in its Creator and Lord" (*Spiritual Exercises*, Rules for Discernment, 316).

Scripture

"Then Jesus answered her, 'Woman, great is your faith! Let it be done for you as you wish.' And her daughter was healed instantly" (Matthew 15:28).

"And just then some people were carrying a paralyzed man lying on a bed. When Jesus saw their faith, he said to the paralytic, 'Take heart, son; your sins are forgiven'" (Matthew 9:2).

"The apostles said to the Lord, 'Increase our faith!'" (Luke 17:5).

"I have prayed for you that your own faith may not fail; and you, when once you have turned back, strengthen your brothers" (Luke 22:32).

"Later he appeared to the eleven themselves as they were sitting at the table; and he upbraided them for their lack of faith and stubbornness, because they had not believed those who saw him after he had risen" (Mark 16:14).

"For we walk by faith, not by sight" (2 Corinthians 5:7).

"For in Christ Jesus . . . the only thing that counts is faith working through love" (Galatians 5:6).

"For by grace you have been saved through faith, and this is not your own doing; it is the gift of God" (Ephesians 2:8).

Further Resources

Matthew 8:10, 13

2 Corinthians 13:5

Galatians 2:20

Hebrews 11:1

Hebrews 12:2

Reflection Questions

CONSIDERATIONS FOR PRAYER

- Has my understanding of faith moved from being only an acceptance of truths to a trusting relationship with God as a person?

- What have the major decisions of my life said about my faith?

- Am I aware of a shift to making assessments about life not only from a human perspective but also from a faith perspective?

- In what area of my life is my faith being challenged? What am I doing with the doubts that I have?

DISCERNMENT WITHIN A RELATIONSHIP

- Who are my friends in faith?

- Who has modeled a faith-filled life for me?

- How strong is my faith in God's action in the lives of other people?

- To what strangers has my faith opened me?

DISCERNMENT WITHIN A GROUP

- What role did faith play in bringing us together as a group?

- Do we find opportunities to share faith in a prayerful setting with each other?

- Does our shared experience nourish and challenge our faith?

A DISCERNING RELATIONSHIP WITH THE WORLD

- How much effort am I making to integrate my faith into my decisions and actions regarding family, church, national, and world justice issues?

Vatican Council II

"This synod wishes to set forth the authentic teaching on divine revelation and its transmission. For it wants the whole world to hear the summons to salvation, so that through hearing it may believe, through belief it may hope, through hope it may come to love" (DV 1, 97).

"Before people can come to the liturgy they must be called to faith and to conversion" (SC 9, 122).

"The manifest action of the Holy Spirit is making lay people nowadays increasingly aware of their responsibility and encouraging them everywhere to serve Christ and the church" (AA 1, 403–404).

"All religious, therefore, with undiminished faith, with charity towards God and their neighbor, with love for the cross and with the hope of future glory, should spread the good news of Christ throughout the whole world, so that their witness will be seen by all . . ." (PC 25, 401).

Spirit-Filled

. . . .

Discernment of spirits is a process guided by the Spirit. Jesus Christ, present now through the action and gifts of his Spirit, shows us how to be attentive to, but not burdened by, seeking God's will in daily life. The grace and gift of discernment also helps us to recognize influences which are not of God.

Ignatian Insights

"Once he (Ignatius) was going out of devotion to a church situated a little more than a mile from Manresa . . . and the road goes by the river. As he went along occupied with his devotions, he sat down for a little while with his face toward the river which ran down below. While he was seated there, the eyes of his understanding began to be opened; not that he saw any vision, but understood and learned many things, both spiritual matters and matters of faith and of scholarship and this with so great an enlightenment that everything seemed new to him. The details that he understood then, though there were many, cannot be stated, but only that he experienced a great clarity in his understanding. This was such that in the whole course of his life, after completing sixty-two years, even if he gathered up all the various helps he may have had from God and all the various things he has known, even adding them all together, he does not think he had got as much as at that one time" (*Autobiography*, 30).

"While he was still at Vicenza, he learned that one of the companions, who was at Bassano, was ill to the point of death; at the same time he [Ignatius] too was ill with fever. Nevertheless he set out and walked so vigorously that Faber, his companion could not keep up with him. On that journey he had assurance from God, and he told Faber so, that the companion would not die of that illness. On their arriving at Bassano, the sick man was much comforted and soon recovered" (*Autobiography*, 95).

Grace

To deepen my faith in the Spirit acting within me at this present time and space.

Scripture

"The spirit of the LORD shall rest on him, the spirit of wisdom and understanding, the spirit of counsel and might, the spirit of knowledge and the fear of the LORD" (Isaiah 11:2).

"For wisdom, the fashioner of all things, taught me. There is in her a spirit that is intelligent, holy, unique, manifold, subtle, mobile, clear, unpolluted, distinct, invulnerable, loving the good, keen, irresistible" (Wisdom 7:22).

"The angel said to her, 'The Holy Spirit will come upon you, and the power of the Most High will overshadow you; therefore the child to be born will be holy; he will be called Son of God'" (Luke 1:35).

"This is the Spirit of truth, whom the world cannot receive, because it neither sees him nor knows him. You know him, because he abides with you, and he will be in you" (John 14:17).

"Do not grieve the Holy Spirit of God, with which you were marked with a seal for the day of redemption" (Ephesians 4:30).

"By this we know that we abide in him and he in us, because he has given us of his Spirit" (1 John 4:13).

"The Advocate, the Holy Spirit, whom the Father will send in my name, will teach you everything, and remind you of all that I have said to you" (John 14:26).

Reflection Questions

CONSIDERATIONS FOR PRAYER

- What does it mean to me to be filled with or to experience the Spirit?
- How are the gifts of the Holy Spirit operative in my life?

Further Resources

Isaiah 42:1

Matthew 1:18

Matthew 12:18

John 16:13

Acts 2:17

Acts 4:7–13

Spiritual Exercises 330

AA3, 406

Apostolicam Actuo si tatem

- Have I ever "grieved the Holy Spirit"? How have I recognized this resistance to grace?
- What is my usual reaction to feeling blank, or dry, or confused, or without understanding? Is trust in the Spirit a part of that reaction?
- When have I experienced myself nudged by the Holy Spirit? What was the quality of that experience? How did it differ from having my own "brilliant idea"?
- What patterns and thoughts indicate to me that I am open to the Spirit? Led by the Spirit?

DISCERNMENT WITHIN A RELATIONSHIP

- What environmental conditions seem necessary for me to be attentive to the Spirit in myself and in others?
- What is my reaction when I am in the presence of someone who clearly is attentive to the Spirit?
- In what ways do I reverence the Spirit in another person?

DISCERNMENT WITHIN A GROUP

- Do we ask the Spirit to guide our conversations and deliberations?
- What qualities characterize our interactions when the Spirit is active and heeded?

A DISCERNING RELATIONSHIP WITH THE WORLD

- Am I growing in a consciousness that the Spirit is always creating and re-creating the world?
- What global issues seem to be ones in which the Spirit is crying out for our response as co-creators and collaborators?

Vatican Council II

"Christ is now at work in human hearts by the power of his Spirit; not only does he arouse in them a desire for the world to come but he quickens, purifies, and strengthens the generous aspirations of humanity to make life more humane and [reverencing] the earth for this purpose" (GS 38, 203–204).

"The people of God believes that it is led by the Spirit of the Lord who fills the whole world. Impelled by that faith, they try to discern the true signs of God's presence and purpose in the events, the needs and the desires which it shares with the rest of humanity today" (GS 11, 173).

"The apostolate is lived in faith, hope and charity poured out by the Holy Spirit into the hearts of all the members of the church" (AA 3, 406).

Actions for Justice

In a world crying out for just women and men who do the just thing, discernment must play a critical role. Discernment helps us to be attentive to the movements of consolation and desolation so that we can choose the option for justice that will give glory to God and also keep us grounded in our personal Christian identity.

Ignatian Insights

"In the hospice he began to speak with many who came to visit him, of the things of God, by whose grace much fruit was derived. As soon as he arrived, he decided to teach Christian doctrine every day to children, but his brother strongly objected to this, saying no one would come. He replied that one would be enough. But after he began to do it, many came continually to hear him; and even his brother. Besides Christian doctrine, he also preached on Sundays and feasts, with profit and help to the souls who came many miles to hear him. He also made an attempt to eliminate some abuses (gambling and concubines for priests), and with God's help some were set right. . . . He got an order to be given that the poor should be provided for officially and regularly . . ." (*Autobiography,* 88–89).

"To ask for interior knowledge of all the great good I have received, in order that, stirred to profound gratitude, I may become able to love and serve the Divine Majesty in all things" (*Spiritual Exercises,* 233).

"There is not sufficient time to do everything" (*Spiritual Exercises,* 18).

Grace

To be on the alert for the opportunity to act for justice within the circle of my relationships and influence.

Scripture

"'Before I formed you in the womb I knew you, and before you were born I consecrated you; I appointed you a prophet to the nations.' I said, 'Ah, LORD God! Truly I do not know how to speak, I am only a boy.' The LORD said to me, 'Do not say, "I am only a boy"; you shall go to all to whom I send you, and you shall speak whatever I command you, Do not be afraid of them, for I am with you to deliver you. . . . Now I have put my words in your mouth. See, today I appoint you . . . to pluck up and to pull down, to destroy and to overthrow, to build and to plant'" (Jeremiah 1:4–10).

"The eyes of all in the synagogue were fixed on him. Then he began to say to them, 'Today this scripture has been fulfilled in your hearing.' All spoke well of him and were amazed at the gracious words that came from his mouth. They said, 'Is not this Joseph's son?' He said to them, 'Doubtless, you will quote to me this proverb, "Doctor, cure yourself!" And you will say, "Do here also in your hometown the things that we have heard you did at Capernaum."' And he said, 'Truly I tell you, no prophet is accepted in the prophet's hometown'" (Luke 4:20–24).

"See if you can find one person who acts justly and seeks truth—so that I may pardon Jerusalem" (Jeremiah 5:1).

"Give justice to the weak and the orphan; maintain the right of the lowly and the destitute" (Psalm 82:3).

"If you amend your ways . . . act justly one with another, do not oppress the alien, the orphan, and the widow, or shed innocent blood . . . then I will dwell with you . . . forever and ever" (Jeremiah 7:5–7).

"Do you love me?" And [Peter] said to [Jesus], "Lord, you know everything; you know that I love you." Jesus said to him, "Feed my sheep" (John 21:17).

Further Resources

Amos 5:24

Proverbs 8:20

Isaiah 16:3

Micah 6:8

Matthew 25:37–41, 45

Luke 10:36–37

Reflection Questions

CONSIDERATIONS FOR PRAYER

- Has my justice grown to include mercy and compassion?
- In my concern for justice, how do I move from sentiments and words to faithful action?

DISCERNMENT WITHIN A RELATIONSHIP

- What is my motivation for joining others in actions for justice?
- How do my family and work circumstances call me to act for justice?

DISCERNMENT WITHIN A GROUP

- What have been the implications for justice in the decisions we have made in the last six months?
- Are we becoming more just in our actions?
- What local injustices bother us enough to move us to some action?

A DISCERNING RELATIONSHIP WITH THE WORLD

- What openness do I need in order to understand how injustice can inhabit the systems of which I am a part?
- Is justice the lens I use to view other races, classes, and world events?

"The council proposes to set down the true and noble nature of peace, to condemn the savagery of war, and to encourage Christians to cooperate with all in securing a peace based on justice and charity and in promoting the means necessary to attain it, under the help of Christ, author of peace" (GS 77, 263).

"All people of whatever race, condition or age, in virtue of their dignity as human persons, have an inalienable right to education. This education should be suitable to the particular destiny of the individuals, adapted to their ability, sex, and national cultural traditions . . ." (GE 1, 576).

"The laity accomplish the church's mission in the world principally by that blending of behavior and faith . . . by that uprightness in all their dealings which persuades everyone to love the true and the good . . . by that love which bids them share the living conditions and labors, the sufferings and yearnings of their sisters and brothers, and thereby prepare all hearts, gently, imperceptibly, for the action of saving grace" (AA 13, 421).

Attentive to Facts

Effective discernment is often dependent upon the quality and adequacy of the information that is gathered and reflected upon for the sake of making connections and seeing relationships among facts. With a full understanding of adequate data, the discerning person can make judgements that are appropriate, timely, and just.

Ignatian Insights

"As the pilgrim was about to set out (for his native air), he learned that he had been accused before the inquisitor, with a case brought against him. Knowing this but seeing that they did not summon him, he went to the inquisitor and told him what he had heard. . . . Would he please pass sentence. The inquisitor said it was true there was an accusation, but that he did not find anything of importance in it. . . . Nevertheless, Ignatius again insisted that the case be carried through to the sentence. As the inquisitor excused himself, he (Ignatius) brought a public notary and witnesses to his house, and obtained a testimonial on this whole affair" (*Autobiography*, 86).

"It should be presupposed that every good Christian ought to be more eager to put a good interpretation on a neighbor's statement than to condemn it. Further, if one cannot interpret it favorably, one should ask how the other means it. If that meaning is wrong, one should correct the person with love; and if this is not enough, one should search out every appropriate means through which, by understanding the statement in a good way, it may be saved" (*Spiritual Exercises*, 22).

"The Fifth Point (in making a good and sound election). After I have thus considered and reasoned out all the aspects of the proposed matter, I should see to which side reason more inclines. It is in this way, namely, according to the greater motion

Grace

To be open to gathering and reflecting upon all information that is relevant and available for a decision.

arising from reason, and not according to some motion arising from sensitive human nature, that I ought to come to my decision about the matter proposed" (*Spiritual Exercises*, 182).

Scripture

"Solomon loved the LORD. . . . At Gibeon the LORD appeared to Solomon in a dream by night; and God said, 'Ask what I should give you.' Solomon said, 'You have shown great and steadfast love to your servant my father David, because he walked before you in faithfulness, in righteousness, and in uprightness of heart toward you; and you have kept for him this great and steadfast love, and have given him a son to sit on his throne. And now . . . you have made your servant king in place of my father David, although I am only a little child; I do not know how to go out or come in. Your servant is in the midst of the people whom you have chosen, a great people, so numerous they cannot be numbered or counted. Give your servant therefore an understanding mind to govern your people, able to discern . . .'"(1 Kings 3:3, 5–10).

"I know the plans I have for you, says the LORD, plans . . . to give you a future with hope. When you search for me, you will find me; if you seek me with all your heart, I will let you find me, says the LORD" (Jeremiah 29:11, 13–14).

"I want to know Christ and the power of his resurrection and the sharing of his sufferings. . . . Not that I have already obtained this or have already reached the goal; but I press on to make it my own, because Christ Jesus has made me his own . . . forgetting what lies behind and straining forward to what lies ahead, I press on toward the goal . . . in Christ Jesus. . . . If you think differently about anything, this too God will reveal to you . . . let us hold fast to what we have attained" (Philippians 3:10–16).

Further Resources

Deuteronomy 30:19

1 Corinthians 1:4–9

Nostra Aetate 2

Reflection Questions

CONSIDERATIONS FOR PRAYER

- What are the resources for reliable information which I have learned to use?

- Are there some people to whom I often turn for reliable information?

- Am I faithful to attending to the thoughts and feelings which occur as I consider new information? Do I notice an increase in interior freedom as I do so?

- What do I do when information challenges my prior opinions or convictions?

DISCERNMENT WITHIN A RELATIONSHIP

- Have we learned to share information freely with each other while also respecting the confidentiality required by other relationships?

DISCERNMENT WITHIN A GROUP

- Do we make our decisions based upon full information even when further information may slow our decision making process?

- Are we free enough to ask someone we don't know well for the information we may need?

- Are we open to relevant information that may at first seem foreign to the matter we are discerning?

- In light of our varied gifts, what distinct role does each of us play in gathering, reviewing, and assessing the significance of the information?

A DISCERNING RELATIONSHIP WITH THE WORLD

- How does my use of the media and electronic resources aid or hinder a careful discernment process?

- Am I ready for a discerned decision that may place me in a countercultural stance?

Vatican Council II

"There exists therefore in human society a right to information on matters which are of concern to people either as individuals or as members of society, according to each one's circumstances. The proper exercise of this right demands that the content of the communication be true and—within the limits set by justice and charity—complete, and that it be presented decently and appropriately" (IM 5, 541).

"The search for truth, however, must be carried out in a manner that is appropriate to the dignity and social nature of the human person: that is, by free enquiry with the help of teaching or instruction, communication and dialogue. It is by these means that people share with each other the truth they have discovered, or think they have discovered, in such a way that they help one another in the search for truth. Moreover, it is by personal assent that they must adhere to the truth they have discovered" (DH 3, 554).

THE DISCERNMENT PROCESS:
Discernment as a Way of Life

Because he has given us of his Spirit

Our loving Creator continues to set the pace for our lives by pouring the Spirit's invitations into our human relationships. Because Jesus Christ has promised to give us his Spirit each day, we are blessed with many opportunities to respond with generosity. Discernment truly becomes a way of life in God's Spirit for us. Our challenge is to respond to the movement of the Spirit as other holy people have done.

Take, Lord, and receive all my liberty, my memory, my understanding, and all my will—all that I have and possess. You, Lord, have given all that to me. I now give it back to you, O Lord. All of it is yours. Dispose of it according to your will. Give me love of yourself along with your grace, for that is enough for me.

—IGNATIUS OF LOYOLA

I belong all to God. There is nothing I would not leave to do His holy will and to satisfy Him.

—CORNELIA CONNELLY

Nothing is more practical than finding God, that is, than falling in love in a quite absolute, final way. What you are in love with, what seizes your imagination, will affect everything. It will decide what will get you out of bed in the morning, what you do with your evenings, how you spend your weekends, what you read, who you know, what breaks your heart, and what amazes you with joy and gratitude. Fall in love, stay in love, and it will decide everything.

—ATTRIBUTED TO PEDRO ARRUPE, S. J.

APPENDIX 1

Discernment as a Process for Personal Decision Making

Discernment as a process guides us as we seek to recognize and respond to God's presence and action in our lives and in the world. It requires a twofold attentiveness: to our unfolding relationship with God and to a growing sensitivity of heart and mind to the ways of God. Our relationships with God in prayer, with other persons, and with the world are the life spaces within which this twofold attentiveness grows and develops.

Gradually, this attentiveness makes apparent within us a "profile" of the qualities of a discerning life (cf. Profile of a Discerning Life, page 154). These qualities are critical supports when we are faced with a choice or decision which we recognize as an important moment in our ongoing life response to God. At such a time, we turn to serious prayer about the decision to be made if we want our faith to ground our decision making. We truly want to find and carry out the will of God.

St. Ignatius understood such life choices and sketched out in *The Spiritual Exercises*, a process which offers some guidelines. As we approach such a decision or, in the words of Ignatius, an "election," it is impor-tant to refocus our intention upon the end or purpose of our lives. In that context we will see the significance of our choices.

"In every good election, insofar as it depends on us, the eye of our intention ought to be single. I ought to focus only on the purpose for which I am created, to praise God our Lord and to save my soul. Accordingly, anything whatsoever that I elect ought to be chosen as an aid toward that end. . . . Finally, nothing whatever ought to move me to choose such means or deprive myself of them except one alone, the service and praise of God our Lord and the eternal salvation of my soul" (*Spiritual Exercises*, 169).

Recognizing that there will be various conditions possible within the mind and heart of the decision maker, Ignatius speaks of the "times" in which a major decision or "election" can be made. He distinguishes three different possible "times":

The "First Time" occurs when the person experiences an almost immediate certainty about a decision; awareness of the better choice seems to come from God without a lot of human interaction.

"The First Time is an occasion when God our Lord moves and attracts the will in such a way that a devout person, without doubting or being able to doubt, carries out what was proposed. This is what St. Paul and St. Matthew did when they followed Christ our Lord" (*Spiritual Exercises*, 175).

The "Second Time" refers to the more usual experience when faced with a decision, of having a variety of affective experiences together with the consolation and desolation which they carry. By discerning that one is moved toward a particular decision by God's spirit rather than another spirit, one comes to clarity about a decision.

"The Second Time is present when sufficient clarity and knowledge are received from the experience of consolations and desolations, and from experience in the discernment of various spirits" (*Spiritual Exercises*, 176).

The "Third Time" is one in which one's affectivity is quiet and not affected by movements of consolation or desolation. In such a tranquil condition, Ignatius suggests that the discerner consider the goal and purpose of life and then, through a consideration of the factors both in favor of a particular decision and those which are against a particular decision, move to a conclusion about the best possible choice or decision. One must consider not merely the quantity of factors, but also their weight and quality.

"The third time is one of tranquility. I consider first the end for which human beings are born, namely, to praise God Our Lord and to save their souls; then, desiring this, as the means I elect a life or state of life within the limits of the Church, in order to be helped in the service of my Lord and the salvation of my soul. By a time of tranquility I mean when the soul is not being moved one way and the other by various spirits and uses natural faculties in freedom and peace" (*Spiritual Exercises*, 177).

After acknowledging what our interior experience is, what "time" we are in, we are ready to move forward in the process of discernment. Just as when we are developing a discerning heart, a faith-filled and experienced listener can be a great help to us. The listener may be a spiritual director, a spouse, a good friend, a pastoral leader, a teacher, a doctor, a colleague. Any person of faith may fill that role, but it is important that the person be one with the time to devote to reflective conversation, the interior freedom and the capacity to listen without agendas, the capacity to pose questions that will enhance our exploration of the material related to our decision.

While that person will not do our discerning for us, much less make the decision for us, he or she will need to be carefully discerning about his or her own experience of consolation and desolation, and of interior freedom. The listener's attentiveness will help us to be more attentive. Thus he or she will contribute both the necessary objectivity and wisdom to the process.

While there are some specific steps to be taken in a formal discernment process, one's growth in the interior freedom to be available to God's action will be an ongoing experience. It need not surprise us if, as we move through the discernment, the process seems to pause when we are challenged by God to deeper levels of interior freedom, perhaps in areas or about matters that surprise us. It is as if God who dwells in full light is intent upon clearing the fog from our minds and the glue from our hearts so that we can see and even feel the way in which God is leading us into God's light on the matter to be decided. Pausing in the steps of the process to seek greater interior freedom when it becomes apparent that we need it never halts the process; it is part of the process.

At times, we will need honesty to surrender to the realization that we do not bring as much freedom to the decision as we would like. We ask God to work through our limits or at least not to let them block our finding God's will for us. We may need to trust that God will have brought us to the requisite interior freedom and clarity of mind and heart by the time the decision needs to be made—and often, not a moment sooner! Progressively throughout the process, it will become evident to us and to our faith companion whether we have the interior freedom which is necessary for us to move to the next step of the process.

With as much interior freedom as possible, we are ready to consider all the data related to the option before us. A full and free consideration of all the data and options will require necessary perspective and objectivity. Carrying out the steps in a discernment process takes time. Without that time, it might be better to use another mode of prayerful decision making. Even though remotely prepared by our repeated choices to develop a discerning heart, we are called to trust God's action as we move through each step of the process even if it takes more time than we had expected. Ideally, our prior ongoing efforts to develop the qualities of a discerning person will bear fruit at this point when we are faced with a concrete decision.

The steps involved in discerning a particular decision seem to unfold in the following sequence:

1. Naming of the question, option, problem, issue about which one wants to discern God's will at this time in one's life.

- What is the matter about which I want to engage in a discernment process?

- Is it of enough significance for me or others to warrant the time and energy which such a process will require?

- Am I sure that I am not planning to use discernment as a way of denying a reality which confronts me?

- If another person asked me to engage in this discernment process, was it appropriate for them to do so?

- Am I sure that the decision is mine to make?

- Are there other people who must be involved with me in the decision making?

- What place will their input have in my decision?

- Has my naming of the issue resulted, at least in part, from my prayer about the matter?

"I should beg God Our Lord to be pleased to move my will and to put into my mind what I ought to do in regard to the matter proposed, so that it will be more to his praise and glory" (*Spiritual Exercises*, 180).

2. Developing the necessary interior freedom and detachment from one's biases in order to be open to the action of God.

- Having named the matter to be discerned, in what areas do I find myself in need of more interior freedom?

- What aspects of my life will be affected by this decision? How do I feel about that?

- Am I free enough to accept whatever consequences will flow from the decision?

- What fears and doubts are stirred in me by this matter? Are they proportionate to the importance of the decision? What might that be telling me?

- What hopes and joys are stirred in me by this matter? Are they realistic and proportionate to the potential of the decision? What might that be telling me?

- Recall the memory of past good decisions. Is there congruence between my present consolation-desolation and what I experienced in the past good decisions?

3. Gathering and attending to the hard data of facts.

Thoughts and feelings in response to the data will occur in the discerner as well as in those people involved in the matter to be decided. Focused prayer about the facts and data will help one to stay free and grounded in one's own decision making process.

- Have I sought out people and other resources which can give me solid, objective information about the matter?

- What factors do I wish were not part of the matter? What feelings do they surface within me? What do I need to do with the feelings?

- If family members, colleagues, neighbors, or other associates will be affected by my decision, have I consulted with them?

- What have their responses revealed to me? What significance or weight do I need to give to that information?

- Do I understand what will be involved in carrying out the decision?

"I should beg to accomplish this by reasoning well and faithfully with my intellect, and by choosing in conformity with his most holy will and good pleasure" (*Spiritual Exercises*, 180).

4. Framing a statement of the decision, action, issue to be discerned in such a way that one can view the option from the vantage point of its pros and its cons.

By using one's reason to name and consider the things in favor, "the pros," and the things against a particular decision, "the cons," one lists all the factors of which one is aware.

- Am I able to state simply the matter to be discerned?
- What are all the "cons" or factors which seem to be against the particular decision?
- What are all the "pros" or factors which seem to be in favor of the particular decision?
- As I prayerfully consider the weight of the "cons" and the "pros" to the particular decision, what do I discover?
- What does my experience of consolation and desolation at this time add to my understanding of how I am being led by God?

"I should consider and reason out how many advantages or benefits accrue to myself from having the [matter] proposed, all of them solely for the praise of God our Lord and the salvation of my soul and on the contrary I should similarly consider the disadvantages and dangers in having it. Then . . . I should consider the advantages and benefits in not having it, and contrarily the disadvantages and dangers in not having it" (*Spiritual Exercises*, 181).

5. Attending to the interior movement of God.

- Will this decision be in harmony with my vocational identity? Does it seem to fit with the person I know myself to be or to be becoming?
- Does it draw me more deeply into union with God in the same kind of way that other good decisions have done?
- What is my experience of consolation and desolation at this stage in the process?
- In light of experiencing these movements, where do the weightier factors seem to fall?

"After I have thus considered and reasoned out all the aspects of the proposed matter, I should see to which side reason more inclines. It is in this way, namely, according to the greater motion arising from reason, and not according to some motion arising from sensitive human nature, that I ought to come to my decision about the matter proposed" (*Spiritual Exercises*, 182).

6. Additional help when needing more clarity.

Ignatius suggests three simple considerations that may bring more clarity to our process.

"I will imagine a person whom I have never seen or known. Desiring all perfection for him or her, I will consider what I would say in order to bring such a one to act and elect for the greater glory of God our Lord and the greater perfection of his or her soul. Then, doing the same for myself, I will keep the rule which I set up for another" (*Spiritual Exercises*, 185).

"I will consider, as if I were at the point of death, what procedure and norm I will at that time wish I had used in the manner of making the present election. Then, guiding myself by that norm, I should make my decision on the whole matter" (*Spiritual Exercises*, 186).

"Imagining and considering how I will find myself on judgment day, I will think how at that time I will wish I had decided in regard to the present matter. And the rule which I will then wish I had followed is what I shall apply now, in order that then I may be in complete contentment and joy" (*Spiritual Exercises*, 187).

- What new awareness about the choice before me results from using my imagination this way?

- What new perspective and understanding have I gained from using these considerations?

7. Offering the decision to God in prayer.

"When that election or decision has been made, the person who has made it ought with great diligence to go to prayer before God our Lord and to offer him that election, that the Divine Majesty may be pleased to receive and confirm it, if it is conducive to his greater service and praise" (*Spiritual Exercises*, 183).

"I shall make my election and offer it to God our Lord . . ." (*Spiritual Exercises*, 188).

"That love which moves me and brings me to choose the matter in question should descend from above, from the love of God; in such a way that the person making the election should perceive beforehand that the love, whether greater or less, which he or she has for the matter being chosen is solely for the sake of our Creator and Lord" (*Spiritual Exercises*, 184).

- What is my experience of consolation and desolation as I offer this decision to God?

8. Seeking confirmation of the decision.

It is at this stage that one's experience of consolation and desolation can also serve to confirm the rightness of a decision. In situations in which one must submit the result of one's discernment to an authority, the confirmation comes in that authority's acceptance of the decision. The lack of confirmation may send one back to an earlier stage in the process—perhaps for a new framing of the matter to be discerned, for more interior freedom, for more data or facts or for a different decision. Any faith choice carries risk, but the risks which God invites us to take will always be blessed by a resulting sense of God's presence and promise to sustain us in living out the choice we have made.

Appendix 2

Abbreviations

The following are the abbreviations of the Constitutions, Decrees, and Declarations of Vatican Council II as they appear sequentially in *Finding God in Each Moment*. The full title of a text is cited the first time the text is quoted. Later citations use only the abbreviation.

The quotations are from *Vatican Council II, A Completely Revised Translation in Inclusive Language*, General Editor Austin Flannery, O.P., Costello Publishing Company, Northport, New York.

GS *Gaudium et spes*: Pastoral Constitution on the Church in the Modern World.

NA *Nostra aetate*: Declaration on the Church's Relations with Non-christian Religions.

AA *Apostolicam actuositatem*: Decree on the Apostolate of the Laity.

CD *Christus Dominus*: Decree on the Pastoral Office of Bishops in the Church.

LG *Lumen gentium*: Dogmatic Constitution on the Church.

SC *Sacrosanctum concilium*: Constitution on the Liturgy.

IM *Inter mirifica*: Decree on the Media of Communication.

DV *Dei verbum:* Dogmatic Constitution on Divine Revelation.

UR *Unitatis redintegratio*: Decree on Ecumenism.

DH *Dignitatis humanae*: Declaration on Religious Liberty.

PO *Presbyterorum ordinis*: Decree on the Life and Ministry of Priests.

AGD *Ad gentes divinitus*: Decree on the Church's Missionary Activity.

PC *Perfectae caritatis*: Decree on the Up-to-date Renewal of Religious Life.

The numbers used in citing *The Spiritual Exercises* and *The Autobiography* refer to the paragraph numbers in the text.

CAROL ANN SMITH, SHCJ, a spiritual director and retreat guide, has extensive experience with Ignatian spirituality, which has shaped her ministries of preparing spiritual directors in the Diocese of Toledo, Ohio, and encouraging lay people in their faith development. She served as director of the Center for Ignatian Spirituality at Marquette University for ten years. She is a member of the Society of the Holy Child Jesus and holds graduate degrees from Villanova University and Catholic University of America.

EUGENE F. MERZ, SJ, a Jesuit, has offered spiritual direction and retreats based on *The Spiritual Exercises of St. Ignatius* and given Ignatian Spirituality workshops around the world for laity, priests, and religious men and women. His years of ministry within the Society of Jesus, in the Diocese of Des Moines, Iowa, and also at the Center for Ignatian Spirituality, have focused upon the spiritual renewal of priests, religious, and laity that was encouraged by Vatican Council II. Merz holds graduate degrees from St. Louis University.

Smith and Merz are the authors of the widely acclaimed *Moment by Moment: A Retreat in Everyday Life*, a groundbreaking book that made the retreat process of *The Spiritual Exercises of St. Ignatius* available to a wide audience for use in homes, parishes, and many other settings. Like *Finding God in Each Moment*, it was based on their years of experience in accompanying others on their faith journey.

Moment by Moment won First Place for First-Time Author in the 2001 Catholic Press Association Awards.

Ignatian Spirituality

Opening to God

A Guide to Prayer
Thomas H. Green, S.J.
An updated edition of a timeless classic. For over thirty-four years, **Opening to God** has de-mystified prayer, explaining what prayer is all about and offering techniques that ready the soul to encounter God.
ISBN: 1-59471-071-6 / 128 pages / $10.95 / Ave Maria Press

Moment by Moment

A Retreat in Everyday Life
Carol Ann Smith, SHCJ & Eugene F. Merz, SJ
Drawing on the classic retreat model, *The Spiritual Exercises of St. Ignatius*, **Moment by Moment** offers a new and inviting way to find God in our often busy and complex lives. Its simple format can be used by an individual or by groups.
ISBN: 0-87793-945-4 / 96 pages / $12.95 / Ave Maria Press

THE IGNATIAN IMPULSE SERIES

Brief, readable, engaging books that present the spirituality of St. Ignatius as a practical resource for spiritual seekers of all faiths.

Seek the Face of God

Discovering the Power of Your Images of God
Karl Frielingsdorf, S.J.
ISBN 1-59471-037-6 / 128 pages / $9.95 / Ave Maria Press

The Sevenfold Yes

Affirming the Goodness of Our Deepest Desires
Willi Lambert, S.J.
ISBN 1-59471-034-1 / 128 pages / $9.95 / Ave Maria Press

The Art of Discernment

Making Good Decisions in Your World of Choices
Stefan Kiechle, S.J.
ISBN 1-59471-035-X / 128 pages / $9.95 / Ave Maria Press

Summoned at Every Age

Finding God in Our Later Years
Peter van Breemen, S.J.
ISBN 1-59471-036-8 / 128 pages / $9.95 / Ave Maria Press

ave maria press

Available from your local bookstore or from **ave maria press** / Notre Dame, IN 46556 / www.avemariapress.com / ph: 1.800.282.1865 / fax: 1.800.282.5681
Prices and availability subject to change.

Keycode: F0A050600000